Introduction to

R[illegible]es

A basic outline of law, procedure, practice and sentencing as it affects road traffic offences dealt with by magistrates' courts in England and Wales, produced under the auspices of the Justices' Clerks' Society.

Introduction to **Road Traffic Offences**

Published 1998 by
WATERSIDE PRESS
Domum Road
Winchester SO23 9NN
Telephone or Fax 01962 855567
INTERNET:106025.1020@compuserve.com

Produced under the auspices of the Justices' Clerks' Society

ISBN Paperback 1 872 870 51 1

Cataloguing-in-Publication Data A catalogue record for this book can be obtained from the British Library

Printing and binding Antony Rowe Ltd, Chippenham

Introduction to

Road Traffic Offences

Winston Gordon
Philip Cuddy
Andy Wesson

The Sentence of the Court Series

Under the auspices of the
Justices' Clerks' Society

Series Editor: Bryan Gibson

WATERSIDE PRESS
WINCHESTER

Winston Gordon is Justices' Clerk, Justices' Chief Executive and Training Officer for Tameside, Greater Manchester. He is a member of the Executive Committee of the Justices' Clerks' Society Standing Committee of Magistrates' Training Officers and of the Duchy of Lancaster Branch Training Committee. He is a solicitor—with experience of advocacy—a tutor at Continuing Professional Development courses and co-author of *The Sentence of the Court, Introduction to the Youth Court* and *Introduction to the Family Proceedings Court*.

Philip Cuddy is Justices' Clerk and Justices' Chief Executive for Stockport, Greater Manchester. He is a solicitor and has held four separate appointments as Justices' Clerk. As Training Officer he has contributed to magistrates and staff training events in many different regions. He is a member of the Standing Committee of Magistrates' Training Officers and co-author of *Introduction to the Youth Court.*

Andy Wesson is Justices' Clerk for the South Bedfordshire magistrates' courts. He is a solicitor and a member of the Criminal Law Network of the Justices' Clerks' Society, and occasional contributor to the weekly journal *Justice of the Peace* and has been a Training Officer for both magistrates and court staff. He was a lecturer on Criminal Procedure on the Court Clerk Diploma Course in London from 1982 to 1985 and continues to be a regular trainer of magistrates and staff.

Bryan Gibson is managing editor of Waterside Press.

Introduction to

Road Traffic Offences

CONTENTS

Abbreviations and Terms used in this Handbook

DVLA Driver and Vehicle Licensing Agency
Excess alcohol Various drink-driving offences: *Chapter* 3
GATSO Speed gun or camera
kgs Kilograms
LGV Large Goods Vehicle
MCA Magistrates' Courts Act, eg MCA 1980
MIB Motor Insurers Bureau
MOT Ministry of Transport (usually MOT test certificate)
Muniquip Speed gun or camera
PACE Police and Criminal Evidence Act 1984
PCV Passenger carrying vehicle
RTA Road Traffic Act (e.g. 1988, 1991)
RTOA Road Traffic Offenders Act 1988
SI Statutory Instrument (also called 'delegated legislation')
TIC Other offences *taken into consideration* when sentencing: *Chapter 9*
VASCAR Visual average speed computer and recorder
VDRS vehicle defect rectification scheme
VEL Vehicle excise licence

Law Reports and Case References

All ER All England Law Reports
Crim. LR Criminal Law Review
RTR Road Traffic Reports
WLR Weekly Law Reports

Fine Values: A Note

All fine values given in this handbook are those applicable as at the time of writing in May 1998 and may be subject to increase from time to time: 🕮☝

Aims and Objectives

Introduction to Road Traffic Offences was compiled under the auspices of the Justices' Clerks' Society by three experienced training officers to magistrates. The aims are:

- to provide a companion for magistrates
- to provide background material for use in training
- to provide an accessible reference point
- to provide information for other court users, students and members of the public about how decisions are made in road traffic cases dealt with by magistrates
- to produce a lucid account, avoiding jargon and complexity. Statutory and other references—the province of court legal/judicial advisers and other lawyers—have been reduced to a minimum.

Important note

The information contained in *Introduction to Road Traffic Offences* cannot replace legal/judicial advice, which should be sought *in all but the most straightforward cases.*

Within the text, the 'helping hand' symbol serves to indicate complex areas of law where magistrates should proceed with extra caution and seek further explanation/advice locally.

The 'helping hand' symbol is as follows: 🕮✋

Acknowledgments

In writing *Introduction to Road Traffic Offences* we are indebted to various people and in particular to George Tranter, Chairman of the Road Traffic Committee of the Justices' Clerks' Society for reading the handbook in draft and making valuable comments. We are also pleased that the Society agreed to lend its general support to this project and allowed it to be developed under its auspices. This is the fourth such handbook to have been completed in this way since 1995, the existing ones being *The Sentence of the Court* (now in its second edition), *Introduction to the Youth Court* and *Introduction to the Family Proceedings Court*.

We are also grateful to the Magistrates' Association for allowing the Road Traffic section of their *Sentencing Guidelines* to be reproduced as an appendix. Our special thanks are also due to Greater Manchester Police for their assistance with *Chapter 6* and to the proprietors of the weekly journal *Justice of the Peace* for allowing us to reproduce an informative article, *Mobile Phones and Road Accidents* as an appendix.

Winston Gordon
Philip Cuddy
Andy Wesson

May 1998

CHAPTER 1

Introduction and General Outline

The police take action against millions of alleged road traffic offenders every year. As a result, numerically speaking, magistrates' courts deal with far more cases involving contravention of the laws affecting the ownership and use of motor vehicles than any other single category of offence. In many instances, lesser offences are dealt with in a matter of seconds, including under statutory procedures whereby people can plead guilty in writing. At the opposite extreme, if a complex defence is put forward, a traffic case can involve extensive evidence and intricate legal considerations, with the outcome—if the matter subsequently results in an appeal to the High Court—affecting many thousands of similar cases across the country.

Road traffic law is, in fact, an immense subject. There is a multitude of offences created by various Acts of Parliament and delegated legislation (statutory instruments or 'SIs') and this is augmented by a vast amount of case law. Similarly, the character of road traffic offences extends from the relatively minor to the very serious indeed, so that broad knowledge and understanding is required of a range of matters.

This handbook has been written in order to highlight common aspects of road traffic offences which are a regular feature in the magistrates' court. It aims to present a straightforward account, whilst explaining some common situations and problems in greater detail. Where there are potential hazards and a need for further, legal/judicial advice locally, this is signified by use of the 'helping hand' symbol which is as follows: 📖✋

WHAT ARE 'ROAD TRAFFIC OFFENCES'?

Strictly speaking, there is no such thing as a road traffic offence. Speeding, parking on double yellow lines and careless driving are just as much *crimes* as are theft, assault or even murder: the law draws no fundamental distinction and courts follow the same procedures and rules of evidence as they do with other crimes. But there *are* refinements and special aspects—discussed in this and later chapters—which tend to set traffic offences apart. Also, in most instances traffic offences do not require any special mental element (*mens rea:* see under the sub-heading *Absolute offences* later in this chapter). There is also the possibility of an administrative penalty such as a 'fixed penalty' for certain offences: *Chapter 9.*

A distinction of convenience

Any distinction is thus largely one of convenience, and made for much the same reason that some courts schedule 'traffic courts', that there are specialist text books and law reports—and that, e.g. the Magistrates' Association devotes a separate section within its *Sentencing Guidelines* to 'Road Traffic Offences': see *Appendix A* to this handbook. Items such as the rules affecting endorsement of penalty points on a driving licence, disqualification from driving, the special rules and obligations placed on vehicle owners and drivers, common definitions, and considerations affecting, say, offences relating to the construction and use of motor vehicles dictate that road traffic matters should be studied and considered separately.

Similar questions might be asked about where this distinction of convenience ends. Some offences committed with a motor vehicle would immediately be thought of as 'crimes proper', not just offences which happen to relate to or involve a motor vehicle. Both murder and manslaughter have been committed by using a car as a weapon and robberies or smuggling operations regularly involve the use of a vehicle. None of these would be thought of as road traffic offences, but other offences may be more closely related, even if the connection, legally speaking, may be somewhat tenuous. This in-between area is dealt with in *Chapter 5, Theft, Taking Vehicles and Like Matters.*

What must be emphasised is that the same high judicial, evidential and legal standards apply, whatever the nature of the offence. A serious offence is no less serious because it involves the use of a motor vehicle. Some traffic offences such as those involving drink, drugs or dangerous driving can be extremely serious: see *Chapter 9.*

SCHEME OF THE HANDBOOK

The rest of this chapter deals with items which are of a general nature, including definitions, jurisdiction, evidence and some procedures. The scheme of the handbook is then as follows:

- *Chapter 2* deals with *Dangerous and Careless Driving* and the obligations which arise when an accident occurs
- *Chapter 3* focuses on *Offences Involving Drink or Drugs,* the former, sadly, being a regular feature of the business of magistrates' courts since the introduction of the breathalyser
- all motorists must hold a driving licence, be insured, their vehicles must be taxed (by obtaining and paying for what is called a 'vehicle excise licence') and the vehicle in question must, if at least three years old, have a current Ministry of Transport

certificate (MOT), the subject of *Chapter 4, Legal Obligations and Documentation* which also deals with fraud concerning such items

- as already indicated, *Chapter 5* deals with *Theft, Taking Vehicles and Like Matters*—including tampering with motor vehicles and the relatively recently created offence of aggravated vehicle taking
- *Chapter 6* covers a selection of *Miscellaneous Offences:* driving whilst disqualified, speeding, failing to comply with traffic signals and pedestrian or school crossing regulations, leaving a vehicle in a dangerous position, obstruction of the highway, motorway offences and the offences arising from the regulations relating to the construction and use of motor vehicles and drivers' hours (the so-called 'tachograph' laws)
- *Chapters 7* and *8* deal with what may matter most to many motorists, the *Endorsement and Penalty Points* provisions and *Disqualification From Driving,* the former chapter also dealing with the relatively novel provisions under which the licence of a newly qualified driver may be revoked at an early stage in his or her driving career if they start to accumulate penalty points
- *Chapter 9* deals with the sentencing of offenders and seeks to draw together a number of considerations affecting traffic offences against the general background of sentencing law.

These chapters are supplemented by appendices dealing more closely with specific aspects (see page v). Whilst it would be quite impossible, in a handbook of this kind, to cover everything which a magistrate or practitioner might meet in court on a busy day, this collection of regular items, broadly described, should enable further information, advice and explanations to be sought with confidence.

DEFINITIONS AND TERMINOLOGY

Since road traffic law is mainly created by Acts of Parliament, there is a need to look at individual statutory provisions and to consider the words used in relevant legislation—and sometimes to look at case law to discover the meaning of a word or phrase. Such meanings are fundamental to an understanding of whether an offence may have been committed or to what sentence or order can or should occur. There is, e.g. a difference between a *motor vehicle* and a *mechanically propelled vehicle* and, again, between these and a *conveyance.* Similarly, there is a difference between *use* of a motor vehicle, *driving* and *being in charge.*

Some commonly recurring definitions

Where definition or interpretation in a given context is not straightforward—then advice should be always be sought: 🕮 ✋. The following items give some impression of the kind of technical considerations which may need to be borne in mind, certainly where they are in issue and often in otherwise quite straightforward cases.

Accident

The High Court has suggested the following:

> Would an ordinary man, in the circumstances of the case, say there had been an accident?

There is no need for two vehicles for there to be an accident—a telegraph pole will do! Property may have been damaged, or worse, a pedestrian. The powers of the police may depend on whether there has been an accident—as under the breath testing legislation.

Mechanically propelled vehicle

This is the term used in prosecutions for dangerous and careless driving offences. It includes any vehicle with mechanical transmission of power from the engine to the wheels, no matter how the engine is driven—whether by diesel, petrol, oil, electricity or steam.

It would embrace such vehicles as an electrically assisted pedal cycle, a milk float, a steam roller, and even a dumper truck. However, whilst all motor vehicles are mechanically propelled vehicles, the converse may not always be true. In one case, a car which had no engine was still held to be a mechanically propelled vehicle as there was a prospect that the engine would be replaced in a reasonable time. The onus is on the prosecutor to show that the particular vehicle has not reached a stage where it can be said that there is no reasonable prospect of it ever being mobile again.

Motor vehicle

Generally, this means a mechanically propelled vehicle *intended or adapted for use on roads*. It should be noted that in respect of a vehicle excise licence, a motor vehicle means a mechanically propelled vehicle *used or kept on any public road*. Thus, even if it is not intended or adapted for use on the roads, an offence may still be committed.

Road

A 'road' means any highway and any other road to which the public has access and includes bridges over which a road passes. Whether a highway is a road is a matter of fact and degree. It has a wider concept than 'highway'. It has been held to include a market place and in some circumstances a car park. In a modern case, the regular and incontrovertible use of a car park as a pedestrian route to a parade of shops was held to be sufficient for the route to qualify as a road.

The prosecutor must prove that it is a 'road' within the meaning of the particular legislation with which the court is concerned. The questions to be addressed are:

- Is the location a definite way between two points where a vehicle can pass?
- Do the general public have access—at least by tolerance—of the owner of the land over which the road passes?

Public road
One repairable at public expense.

Highway
Whilst narrower in concept than a road, the definition of 'highway' includes public bridleways, public footpaths, carriageways, public footways and public driftways. It includes bridges and tunnels over or through which it passes. Anything that can be said to be a highway is also a road. Highways are anywhere the public has a right to pass and re-pass, either on foot, or riding or accompanied by a beast of burden or with vehicles and cattle, as the case may be.

Public place
This means a place to which the public has access. Accordingly, in a leading case on drink driving, it was held that a public house car park was a public place within general licensing hours (i.e. when the public house was entitled to open for the sale of alcohol). In another case it was held that a school playground could be a public place when school has finished for the day. In a recent case an off-road 'parking bay' was held to be a public place. Magistrates may use their own local knowledge in deciding whether a place is a public place. However, the onus remains with the prosecutor to prove that the place is a public place at the time of the offence.

Terminology
It is essential to be familiar with various expressions of a legal or quasi-legal nature, which the following are examples:

Absolute offence (or strict liability)
This means that the offender is liable irrespective of his state of mind. *Mens rea* (or 'guilty intention': below) is not required. Most minor road traffic offences are offences of strict liability. It does not matter *why* someone parked illegally or drove beyond the speed limit (although the explanation *may* amount to a reason for mitigating the normal penalty; for reducing the fine below the local guideline). Most criminal offences have two distinct features:

- an *actus reus*—loosely translated as 'the act itself'. An example might be the act of driving through traffic signals on red.
- *mens rea*—loosely translated as 'the guilty mind'. Hence in an offence of theft of a motor vehicle, part of the *mens rea* would be the element of 'dishonesty'. By contrast, driving through a red light does not require *mens rea.*

As already indicated, many road traffic offences are absolute offences. The prosecutor need only prove the *actus reus*. Where someone drives through a red traffic signal, all the prosecutor has to prove is that the defendant drove through the signal whilst it was on red. Whilst the mental element may have no bearing on whether the offence has been committed and thus whether or not the alleged offender should be convicted, it does have relevance to sentencing. It should be noted that some offences, whilst not requiring *mens rea* in the full sense, do require that the defendant's actions must have fallen below a certain standard. Examples are careless driving and dangerous driving: *Chapter* 2.

Attempting to drive

Generally this means doing an act in relation to the driving of a vehicle which is more than merely preparatory to driving, for example sitting in the driver's seat and trying to start it with a bunch of keys.

Driving

The use of the driver's controls for the purpose of directing the movement of a vehicle. Thus, if a vehicle is being pushed, this may amount to driving. The engine need not be turned on. In one case, the 'steersman' of a towed vehicle was held to be driving. The man was sitting in the cab of a lorry towed by means of a rigid bar which was attached in a flexible fashion to both vehicles. Because of this method, anyone left holding the steering wheel had substantial potential for directional control. The man was convicted of dangerous driving and driving without the required licence (*Whitfield v. Director of Public Prosecutions*, 13 November 1997, Divisional Court, unreported). In another modern case, a passenger decided to frighten a friend who was walking on the pavement. The passenger grabbed the steering wheel and pulled the car towards the pedestrian. On the facts, it was held that though interfering with the driving, he was not actually driving (*Director of Public Prosecutions v. Hastings* [1993] RTR 205).

It is always a question of fact, dependent on the degree and extent of control over the direction and movement of the vehicle.

Using

In some cases 'using' a vehicle may include driving, but this is not always the case. Using connotes a degree of control, management or operation of a vehicle. An example would be using without insurance which does not require the vehicle to have been driven. On the other hand, if the vehicle was driven without insurance by an employee acting in the course of his or her employment by a partnership, all the partners could be prosecuted for using the vehicle without insurance (assuming it was owned by the partnership and was uninsured).

A vehicle has been held to be 'in use' on a road whilst immobile for almost seven months with the rear brakes seized, tyres deflated and gear box containing no oil. The fact that it could not be immediately driven or towed was irrelevant—it was still being used without insurance and a current test certificate.

Each offence must be looked at separately—many road traffic offences do not require any mental element as strict liability is imposed and no *mens rea* is necessary (see above).

Causing

This usually requires proof of a mental element (compare 'using'). Hence, in one case, a company had warned its drivers against over-loading the company's vehicles. One driver ignored the warning and the company was prosecuted for *causing* the offence. The conviction was quashed on appeal on the basis that the company had no prior knowledge of the unlawful act. The appeal court applied the ordinary meaning of the word 'causes' .

Permitting

This involves permission, which must be given expressly or by implication. Generally it requires proof of a mental element in the sense that the person permitting must have prior knowledge of the actions of the user. So, if A allows B to drive his or her motor vehicle, he or she has permitted its use. If A's insurance does not cover B's use (e.g. because B did not hold a valid driving licence) then A has committed the offence of permitting the use of an uninsured motor vehicle even if A was under the mistaken belief that B held a valid driving licence.

In charge

This has relevance to 'drink driving' offences and 'driving whilst under the influence of drugs': *Chapter 3*. The leading case is *Director of Public Prosecutions v. Watkins* [1989] RTR 324 where the High Court provided useful guidance on the meaning of 'being in charge' in this context. The court indicated whilst there could be no hard and fast all-embracing test, there were, broadly speaking two distinct classes of case:

- where the defendant was the owner or lawful possessor and had recently driven the vehicle. This person would normally be in charge and the question then arises whether he or she was still in charge or whether they had put the vehicle in someone else's charge. However he or she would not be in charge if in all the circumstances they had ceased to be in actual control and there was no realistic possibility of resuming actual control whilst unfit, e.g. because he or she was in bed at home for the evening or at some distance from the car, or it had been taken by someone else.

- where the defendant was not the owner, lawful possessor or recent driver but was sitting in the vehicle or otherwise involved with it. Here, the question would be whether he or she had assumed being in charge of the vehicle. They would be in charge if whilst unfit they were voluntarily in *de facto* (i.e. actual) control of the vehicle or might be expected imminently to assume control. Whether he or she was in possession of a key that fitted the ignition would be one of the factors to be taken into account.

Statutory declaration

If someone to whom a summons was addressed did not know of it or the proceedings, e.g. where found guilty in his or her absence, they may make a statutory declaration. In practice, this may occur when the court is considering disqualification from driving. The declaration renders the proceedings void, but they can be re-opened. A statutory declaration must be in the prescribed form. A 'solemn declaration' is made before a magistrate and the form is signed by the person making it and the magistrate concerned. Knowingly and wilfully making a false declaration is an offence attracting imprisonment of up to two years in the Crown Court (six months before magistrates) and/or a fine.

Negative averment

Generally, for a prosecution to succeed, the prosecutor must prove all elements of the offence beyond reasonable doubt. However, in relation to certain alleged road traffic 'document offences' there is a reversal of the normal burden of proof—because it would be impossible for the prosecutor to prove their non-existence. In cases involving allegations of 'no insurance' or 'no MOT test certificate', the burden of proof is on the defendant to prove he or she *was* insured or that the vehicle had a current test certificate—usually by producing the appropriate documentation. Where the *burden* is on the defendant, the *standard* is always on a balance of probabilities. Generally, seek advice:📖✋

Printout

This can mean:

- a computer printout showing someone's driving record, including details of endorsements and disqualification (obtained from the Driver and Vehicle Licensing Agency and thus known as a 'DVLA printout'): see the example on page 26.

- the statement/readout/result produced by the breath analysis machine (usually the Intoximeter: but see *Chapter 3*) at a police station and which shows the proportion/percentage of alcohol in someone's breath at the time of the test: see page 56.

MAGISTRATES' COURT JURISDICTION

The jurisdiction will depend on whether the alleged offence is a 'summary offence' or an 'indictable offence' (including offences triable either way). The magistrates' court has jurisdiction to try

- all summary offences committed within the county or commission area. These are usually heard within the petty sessional division where the offences were allegedly committed, although, in some areas, 'traffic courts' have, to an extent, been centralised. There are refinements to the rules where, e.g. an alleged summary offence has begun in one jurisdiction and ended in another: legal advice should be sought if necessary.
- to deal with any indictable offence wherever committed in England and Wales provided that it is also an either way offence and subject to standard procedures concerning plea before venue, mode of trial and any necessary consent from the accused person. There are few purely indictable offences (i.e. only triable at the Crown Court) or either way offences (triable in the Crown Court or magistrates' court subject to the procedures already mentioned) which fall within the ambit of road traffic legislation. Virtually all are summary only offences. For further explanation of the classification of offences and resulting implications, see *The Sentence of the Court* and/or seek advice as necessary:

TIME LIMITS

There is no time limit in respect of indictable offences (unless expressly provided by statute) although there is a possibility of an 'old' offence being dismissed for abuse of process which can, in certain circumstances, include delay in bringing proceedings.

Six months time limit for summary offences
In respect of summary offences (the vast majority of road traffic cases), an information for the issue of process (normally a summons) must be laid within six months. This six months time limit will normally run

from the date of commission of the offence, although in calculating the six months, the actual day on which the offence was committed is not to be included. There are, though, certain offences where proceedings may be brought within a period of time (usually six months) from the date on which the evidence, sufficient in the opinion of the prosecutor to warrant proceedings, came to his or her knowledge. This is subject to an overall time limit of three years after the commission of the offence. Among the offences that are included in this special category are driving whilst disqualified and using an uninsured motor vehicle (or causing/permitting it to be used). A prosecutor must prove that the information was laid in time if this becomes an issue. A certificate completed and signed by the prosecutor is conclusive evidence.

NOTICE OF INTENDED PROSECUTION

In respect of some offences there is a legal requirement that a person who may be prosecuted must be warned of the possible legal action so that it does not come as a surprise to him. This warning should either be given at the time, or the person must be served with a notice of intended prosecution or a summons within 14 days. The offences for which notice of intended prosecution must be given include: dangerous driving; careless and inconsiderate driving; similar offences involving cycling; leaving vehicles in dangerous positions; failing to comply with traffic signs and speeding.

However if, at the time of the offence or immediately after it, an accident occurs owing to the presence on a road of the vehicle in respect of which the offence was committed, the prosecution are not required to give notice of intended prosecution. This distinction is applicable only where the defendant is aware of the accident. In any case, where the defence maintains no notice was given, the onus of proof will be on the defendant on the balance of probabilities.

Service of a written notice on the driver or registered keeper of a vehicle at a last known address will suffice for good service. A *Notice of Intended Prosecution* is reproduced in *Appendix C* to this handbook.

LEGAL AID

Representation through the legal aid system is available for alleged traffic offences, as it is for all criminal offences. However, in practice it is rarely given, since the majority of traffic offences are not seen as serious enough. Most offences do not carry imprisonment and many do not carry an obligatory disqualification from driving. The relevance to disqualification from driving is that it can have serious consequences, e.g. the ability to earn a living.

Legal aid may be granted if the court is satisfied that the applicant's means are such that he or she requires assistance in paying legal costs in the case and that it is in the interests of justice. It is this latter test which will rule out the grant in the majority of applications for road traffic offences. The factors that are considered include:

- the offence is such that if proved it is likely that the court would impose a sentence which would deprive the accused of his or her liberty or lead to the loss of livelihood or serious damage to reputation
- the determination of the case may involve consideration of a substantial question of law
- the accused may be unable to understand the proceedings or to state his or her own case because of his inadequate knowledge of English, mental illness or other mental or physical disabilities[1]
- the nature of the defence is such as to involve the tracing and interviewing of witnesses, or expert cross-examination of a witness for the prosecution
- it is in the interest of someone other than the accused that the accused be represented.

In *R v. Gravesham Magistrates' Court, ex parte Baker* (1997) *The Times*, 30 April 1997 it was held that it would be appropriate to grant legal aid to a driver who wished to raise a plea of special reasons for not disqualifying (see *Chapter 8*) in relation to an excess alcohol charge. In that case the defendant alleged that his drink had been 'laced' and put forward a cogent argument in support of his application for legal aid; he demonstrated that he would need to call an expert witness and also cross-examine witnesses to the incident.

EVIDENCE

Court hearings of alleged road traffic offences follow the normal rules of evidence. Thus, the same requirements concerning the order of speeches and the giving of evidence apply and, e.g. hearsay will normally be excluded unless it falls within an established exception to the hearsay rule (📖✋) and opinion evidence can only be given by an expert witness and within the limits of that person's expertise (📖✋).

---

1 See, generally, *Interpreters and the Legal Process* by Joan Colin and Ruth Morris, Waterside Press, 1996.

Examples of common *hearsay* situations in relation to traffic offences are:

- things said at the scene of a traffic accident in the absence of the defendant
- registration numbers being passed from one person to another. The second person cannot normally repeat the number in evidence, i.e. for the purpose of proving which car was involved in some incident or other.

Examples of situations where *opinion* evidence may be allowed are as follows:

- speeding cases: see *Chapter 6*
- a forensic examiner giving evidence about the state of a vehicle having first satisfied the court that he or she is an expert for this purpose
- police surgeons expressing medical views.

Again, it must be stressed that this is an area where judicial advice/further explanation is always desirable: 📖✋

Judicial knowledge

Magistrates may use general experience—their 'judicial knowledge'—to draw conclusions. This can sometimes come to the fore in road traffic cases where, e.g. the location or local circumstances may be a factor. So, in one case, it was held that magistrates are entitled to infer that you cannot travel from one part of the town to another in a vehicle unless you used a public highway. Similarly, they are likely to understand that a particular road junction is a notorious 'black spot'. Any 'judicial knowledge' which the justices propose to bring into consideration should be brought to the notice of the parties so that they may make representations or even call evidence.

Local knowledge can be invaluable in interpreting evidence, especially regarding locations, speed limits etc. Magistrates can take 'a view' by visiting a particular location. This is a part of the hearing, so that when they exercise their discretion to visit the scene of an alleged offence magistrates should not do so without the parties also being present. It is possible, e.g. that some special feature of the scene might have altered since the events in question.

Plans

This type of evidence is extremely valuable in some road traffic cases, especially if the plan is drawn to scale. Parties can agree that the draughtsman need not attend the hearing to formally prove the plan.

There are legal rules about the submission of plans as evidence—in particular, notice must be given to the other party. The introduction of 'sketch plans' (especially if not to scale) is more problematic, but these can be admissible: seek legal advice 🕮✋. Similarly, photographs can be admissible (e.g. of the scene of an accident), provided the accuracy of the photograph can be confirmed by evidence. Also, evidence from a roadside 'speed camera' or one set up at traffic lights is admissible subject to special considerations (*Chapter 6*). In some cases, video tapes are now being produced in evidence such as those employed in cameras in police vehicles, and including 'stills' from videos.

Written statements and formal admissions

The statement of a prosecution or defence witness can be produced in evidence under section 9 Criminal Justice Act 1967 without the witness being required to attend court or give evidence in the witness box (testimony) provided certain criteria are satisfied. Such statements are usually referred to as 'section nines'. The written statement must be signed by the person making it and contain a declaration that it is true, together with other prescribed information. The statement will be admissible provided the other party does not object—in accordance with the provisions—within 7 days.

Sometimes inertia on the part of a defendant may mean that he or she does not object within the statutory time limit, but may still attend court and seek to challenge or counter the evidence in the written statement when it is read out in evidence. The court will then need to take account of the overall interests of justice in deciding—notwithstanding the fact that, strictly speaking, the defendant has no right to have the maker of the statement called as a witness—whether to allow an adjournment for this purpose.

A proposed new Act of Parliament (at present The Magistrates' Courts (Procedure) Bill) will allow such statements to be served with the summons, so that the court can proceed to trial at the first hearing if the defendant fails to appear. This is designed to speed up procedures for minor cases such as many road traffic matters, and where the defendant fails to respond to a postal summons.

Under section 10 Criminal Justice Act 1967 either party may formally admit relevant matters so that proof of them in court is no longer required.

Corroboration

Normally evidence which confirms or supports other evidence is not a requirement in relation to most road traffic offences. However, a driver may not be convicted of exceeding the speed limit solely on the *opinion* evidence of one witness. Thus, a policeman on his foot patrol could not be the sole eye witness to a speeding allegation without some corroboration of his evidence. This might, however, be provided by mechanical means, so that, technically only one police officer is required to observe the speedometer of his or her own police car or to operate a 'speed gun' or other speed device: see *Chapter 6* under *Speeding*.

Evidence by certificate (e.g. as to a vehicle driver, user or owner)
In certain circumstances, certificates signed by a police officer which contain admissions by a person specified in the certificate that he or she was the driver, owner or user of a vehicle at a specified time may be received in evidence. Similarly, records held at the DVLA such as registration particulars of vehicles and driving licence details can also be introduced in evidence (usually by way of a validated computer print-out).

A photograph produced by an automatic camera to detect traffic light or speeding offences can be produced in evidence in documentary form, and likewise an Intoximeter printout (*Chapter 3*).

Burden of proof on defendant
Reference has already been made earlier in this chapter to the fact that where a defendant is charged with driving without a licence he or she must prove that they do in fact hold a licence (see under *Negative averment*). A defendant who is before the court facing an allegation of being in charge of a motor vehicle with excess alcohol has a statutory defence if he or she proves they were not likely to drive whilst having excess alcohol in their breath, blood or urine (see, generally, *Chapter 3*). This defence must be proved by him or her, rather than be disproved by the prosecutor. The defendant will need to establish this statutory defence on the balance of probabilities. In other words, he or she must show that it is more likely than not that they would not have driven.

In some cases, even though the prosecutor retains the burden of proof, there is an *evidential burden* on the defendant, e.g. where the facts of an accident give rise to an implication that the defendant was driving carelessly. An example might be where, for some unexplained reason, the defendant's vehicle collided with, say, a tree. There will be an evidential burden on the driver to put forward an explanation—or risk being convicted because the events, *prima facie*, indicate carelessness.

COURT PROCESS

Information and summons
Most road traffic proceedings commence with the laying of an information upon which a summons is issued and served on the

defendant. This is essential if the *Guilty By Post: MCA 1980 Section 12* procedures are being adopted by the prosecutor: see next heading.

Arrest and charge

Sometimes when a defendant has been arrested, e.g. for drink driving offences, he or she will be charged by the police and produced in court, in custody, or be bailed by them to appear in court at a later date.

Warrants 📖✋

There are two types of warrant. The first type of warrant is known as a 'warrant in the first instance'. There must be a written information which must be substantiated on oath. This will be applied for on the basis that the alleged offence is an indictable offence or an either-way matter, or that it is punishable with imprisonment, or the address of the offender has not been clarified sufficiently to enable the service of a summons. The golden rule is that a warrant should not be issued where a summons will suffice.

Sometimes a defendant who has been summoned to appear at court fails to do so. Where the court considers it undesirable to proceed in his or her absence, it may consider the issue of a warrant of arrest provided the information has been substantiated on oath. The offence must be punishable with imprisonment or the court, having convicted the defendant, must be considering disqualifying the defendant from driving. In respect of a convicted defendant under consideration for disqualification, proposed legislation will allow the issue of a warrant without the need for evidence on oath.

GUILTY BY POST: MCA 1980, SECTION 12

This is a procedure (albeit not exclusively linked to road traffic offences) whereby a court can accept the written plea of 'guilty' of a defendant in his or her absence. It only applies to summary offences and does not apply to any offence for which the defendant is liable to more than three months imprisonment.

It is likely to be used in the majority of minor motoring prosecutions. A statement of facts—which, if the procedure is used, must be sent to the defendant by the prosecutor—must be read out in full to the court, and the court must not permit any statement to be made by, or on behalf of, the prosecutor, with respect to any facts relating to the offence charged, other than that statement of facts. Similarly, any statement which the defendant wishes to be brought to the attention of the court with a view to mitigation of sentence must be read out by the court clerk/judicial adviser. It is *not* sufficient for those documents to be handed to the bench for the justices to read themselves or for them to be truncated or edited in any way. The strict, prescribed procedure must be observed, even in the most trivial of cases.

A court may not impose any sentence of imprisonment or other form of detention in the defendant's absence. Similarly, a court may not order disqualification without first adjourning the hearing and notifying the defendant of the adjournment and the reason for it.

A claim for costs can be added to the prosecutor's notification, as can a notice to cite previous convictions.

Where the defendant does not accept the invitation to plead guilty by post, then the magistrates will consider adjourning for the evidence to be heard, assuming that the summons has been properly served. The prosecutor may then wish to arrange the service of witness statements pursuant to section 9 Criminal Justice Act 1967 (see above)—assuming that they have not already been served—which, in the absence of an objection by the defendant, will avoid the need to call the witnesses.

When the defendant does enter a plea of guilty by post (or in person), the court must always be satisfied that the plea is *unequivocal.* In the event of the plea being equivocal, it should not be accepted, e.g. 'I plead guilty to careless driving but it was entirely the other driver's fault'!

RE-OPENING CASES

An appeal can be a costly and time-consuming experience, especially where some pure technicality or irregularity is involved. There are two ways in which this can be avoided.

By way of a statutory declaration

Mention has already been made concerning the possibility of making a statutory declaration where the defendant was unaware of the case. There is a time limit (the declaration must be made within 21 days from a specific date). However, this can be extended: seek advice 🕮✋

Pursuant to section 142 MCA 1980

This useful provision allows the court to re-open the issue of guilt where someone has been found guilty, and the court may vary or rescind a sentence or other order imposed *if it would be in the interest of justice to do so.* Section 142 usually comes into play where a court has proceeded in the defendant's absence and, most typically, he or she has been convicted of document-related offences, e.g. using a motor vehicle without insurance. Regrettably, some defendants do not respond to a summons but, upon receipt of the conviction notice, they go to see a solicitor or attend at the court office with the very document in question. By virtue of section 142 of the 1980 Act, the court can re-open the case, either before the same or different magistrates. This avoids the more costly appeal procedure.

It should be noted that the procedure is not a mere formality and magistrates should consider issues such as why the defendant did not produce the appropriate documents.

Re-opening under section 142 can also be used where the magistrates make a mistake in sentencing, such as where they exceed their powers or wrongly calculate the points and disqualify the driver, who, in fact, was not liable under the 'totting-up' provisions (see *Chapter 8*).

THE HIGHWAY CODE

The *Highway Code* (HMSO) can be invaluable in considering aspects of alleged bad driving. However, failure to comply with the advice or rules of the code is not, in itself, an offence. Hence, a breach will not necessarily result in a conviction—whilst, on the other hand, observing the requirements of the code may not necessarily mean acquittal.

In the normal course of events, the code provides excellent guidance on the standards required for a careful and prudent driver and cyclist. Its provisions often assist magistrates when reaching their decisions as to the facts, and in this sense they are *persuasive* about how a driver should have behaved or reacted in given circumstances.

A new edition of the code (the first since 1993) is expected in the bookshops at the end of 1998. A draft has been released for consultation. One interesting proposal is that motorists must stop their vehicles before making or receiving calls on mobile telephones—even if they have installed 'hands-free' equipment.[2]

---

[2] See also *Mobile Phones and Road Accidents* in *Appendix D* to this handbook.

OTT SUB-BATCH DRIVER AND VEHICLE LICENSING CENTRE SWANSEA
8502 89671NO43 DQ3 REPLY TO ENQUIRIES - POLICE - CERTIFICATES AND DOCUMENTS

ENQ CODE	ENQUIRER /NAME/ADDRESS	DATE	RUN-NO
2000	Nutsford Magistrates' Court Ashton Road, LONDON NW19	01.05.98	619619

> Section 69 and schedule 3 of the Police and Criminal Evidence Act 1984 (does not apply in Scotland); Section 13 of the Road Traffic Offenders Act 1988; Vehicle and Driving Licences Records (Evidence) Regulations 1970.
> As authorised by the Secretary of State I hereby certify that the details in the page(s) of this document is a note of the information contained in the driver licencing records maintained by the Secretary of State for Transport.
> To the best of my knowledge and belief there are no grounds for believing that the statement in the page(s) of this document produced by computer at the Driver and Vehicle Licensing Centre is inaccurate because of improper use of the computer; at all times the computer was operating properly, or if not, any respect in which it was out of operation was not such as to affect the production of the document or the accuracy of its contents.
>
> Maurice Minor
> Service Manager
> DVLC, Swansea

SURNAME Cambridge
FORENAMES Austin
DATE OF BIRTH 13 Jul 1963
SEX Male
INPUT DOC NO 12345

ORIGINAL ENQUIRY CODE 01XU
DATE OF HEARING 31 MAR 1998

REPLY MESSAGE: DETAILS OF RECORD HELD UNDER DRIVER NUMBER (SHEET 1)

NAME AND ADDRESS
- - - - - - - - - -

AUSTIN CAMBRIDGE
DUN SPEEDING
BRANDSHATCH
THRUXTON

PLACE OF BIRTH NOT KNOWN
- - - - - - - - -

OUR RECORDS SHOW THAT THE ABOVE HOLDS NO LICENCE

LICENSING DETAILS
- - - - - - - - - - -

LAST LICENCE ISSUED

ENTITLEMENT NONE HELD

NUMBER OF ENDORSEMENTS (* BELOW)

CONV COURT CODE	DATE OF CONV	OFFE -NCE CODE	DATE OF OFFENCE	FINE	PTS	ALCH LEVEL	DISQUAL PERIOD Y M D	CONCUR	OTHER SENT	PERIOD PRISON SENT SUSP	DISQ TILL T.P.	DATE DISQ REMOVED	DISQ PEND SENT	SENT COURT CODE	DATE OF SENTENCE	DATE DISQUAL SUSPEND	DATE DISQUAL REIMPOSED	APPEAL COURT CODE	REHAB
*2001	15 03 94	LC 20	24 08 93	60.00															
*2001	15 03 94	IN 10	24 08 93	540.00	08														
*2001	21 01 98	SP30	11 09 97	200.00	03														

DOCUMENT TRAIL DETAILS (SHEET 2)

DOCUMENT NUMBER	TYPE OF DOCUMENT
123456789101112	COURT NOTIFICATION
111222333444555	COURT NOTIFICATION
666777888999111	COURT NOTIFICATION

END OF RECORD

Example of a DVLA Printout

CHAPTER 2

Dangerous and Careless Driving (including Accidents)

Every day, people are killed and others seriously injured on the roads as a result of road traffic accidents. Accordingly, there is a likelihood of a wide range of offences being committed as a result of bad driving. In an extreme case (e.g. a motor vehicle being deliberately or recklessly driven at a pedestrian) a charge of murder or manslaughter could result. This type of charge can only be tried in the Crown Court and is not, therefore, the subject of review in this handbook. Suffice it to say that on conviction for 'motor manslaughter' there is a maximum sentence of life imprisonment and/or an unlimited fine. Disqualification from driving is obligatory and there is also the requirement for a re-test.

DANGEROUS DRIVING

The modern law of dangerous driving results from the Road Traffic Act 1991 (which amended the Road Traffic Act 1988). The 1991 Act repealed the existing offence of *reckless* driving. One reason for this was that courts were experiencing difficulties due to the legal definition of recklessness and the subjective considerations involved in deciding if behaviour came within this term. Juries, in particular, experienced problems making decisions about the state of mind of drivers. Hence the new law of *dangerous* driving was based on two main ingredients:

- a standard of driving which fell far below that expected of a competent and careful driver; and
- the notion that the driving should carry a potential or actual danger of physical injury or serious damage to property.

Causing death by dangerous driving

Under section 1 Road Traffic Act 1988 (as amended), someone who causes the death of another person by driving a mechanically propelled vehicle dangerously on a road or other public place is guilty of an offence. The meaning of the terms 'mechanically propelled vehicle', 'road', and 'public place' are mentioned in *Chapter 1*.

The offence of causing death by dangerous driving cannot finally be determined in a magistrates' court and the alleged offender must be committed for trial at the Crown Court if the magistrates, sitting as examining justices, are satisfied that a prima facie case has been made out against the accused.

The maximum penalty is ten years imprisonment and/or an unlimited fine with a minimum disqualification from driving for two years and a compulsory re-test (the extended test: *Chapter 8*).

The offence of dangerous driving

Someone who drives a mechanically propelled vehicle dangerously on a road or other public place is guilty of an offence: section 2 Road Traffic Act 1988 (as amended). Again, terms such as 'mechanically propelled vehicle', 'road', and 'public place' were adverted to in *Chapter 1*.

This is an either-way offence. Thus it may be tried either in the magistrates' court or at the Crown Court. In the magistrates' court it is subject to a maximum sentence of six months imprisonment and/or a fine of £5,000. The Crown Court maxima are two years imprisonment and/or an unlimited fine. Before both courts there must, on conviction, be a minimum 12 months obligatory disqualification (in the absence of special reasons) and a compulsory extended re-test: *Chapters 7* and *8*.

What is dangerous driving?

By virtue of Section 2A Road Traffic Act 1988 (as amended):

> (1) For the purposes of Section 1 and 2 above a person is regarded as driving dangerously if (and, subject to sub section (2) below, only if)
> (a) the way he drives falls far below what would be expected of a competent and careful driver, and
> (b) it would be obvious to a competent and careful driver that driving in that way would be dangerous.
> (2) A person is also to be regarded as driving dangerously for the purpose of sections 1 and 2 above if it would be obvious to a competent and careful driver that driving the vehicle in its current state would be dangerous.

There is thus an objective assessment by the court to decide the standard of a competent and careful driver. So, if the court decides that the driving did not fall *far below* that to be expected of a competent and careful driver, it must acquit the defendant of this offence.

However, if the court does decide that the standard fell far below that to be expected of a competent and careful driver, it would then need to decide whether it would be obvious to a competent and careful driver that driving in that way would be dangerous.

The Court of Appeal has decided that dangerous driving is, in effect, an absolute offence, in the sense that the defendant's knowledge is relevant only in so far as it adds to what would have been obvious to a careful driver; it is not what was obvious to the defendant, but what *should* have been obvious which counts.

State of the vehicle

As indicated above, someone is also to be regarded as driving dangerously if it would be obvious to a careful and competent driver that driving the vehicle in its current state would be dangerous. In determining the state of the vehicle, the court may take into consideration anything attached to it, carried on it or in it, and the manner in which the item is attached or carried. Hence, a driver who should have known that his brakes or steering were defective will, by driving, be liable to conviction for dangerous driving—as will one who drives with an obviously insecure load.

Aggravating and mitigating features of the offence

In adopting a structured approach to sentencing, the following factors have been held to aggravate the offence:

- evidence of alcohol or drugs
- excessive speed
- the fact that the offence was committed whilst on bail
- avoiding detection or apprehension
- competitive driving, racing, showing off
- previous convictions and failing to respond to previous sentences, if relevant
- disregarding warnings from passengers or others in the vicinity
- prolonged, persistent deliberate bad driving.

On the other hand, such features as

- there being only a single incident
- a momentary risk not fully appreciated
- the fact the speed was not excessive
- the fact that no alcohol or drugs were involved

may indicate mitigating features.

Sentencing guidelines

These are among the items and considerations discussed in *Chapter 9*. It is, however, important to appreciate that there are many Court of Appeal decisions concerning death by dangerous driving and dangerous driving. Magistrates should seek appropriate judicial advice in relation to these cases: 📖✋

By way of example, the Court of Appeal has indicated that even a single dangerous event, e.g. a solitary bad manoeuvre on a bend, can result in a custodial sentence. Again, that court has indicated that dangerous driving involving excessive speed over a distance may, where there is death involved, result in a substantial custodial sentence. Even in those cases where there is no serious injury or death involved, it is clear from the tenor of Court of Appeal rulings that where the aggravating features include such factors as excess alcohol or excessive speed over a distance, or the consumption of drugs or deliberate disregard of traffic signals, a custodial sentence should be considered.

Specific examples of dangerous driving

The following factors have been agreed by the Crown Prosecution Service and the police as possibly supporting allegations of dangerous driving (such that prosecutions are the likely outcome):

- any bad driving undertaken deliberately and/or repeatedly
- racing or competitive driving
- prolonged, persistent or deliberately bad driving
- speed which is highly inappropriate for the prevailing road or traffic conditions
- aggressive or intimidatory driving, such as sudden lane changes, cutting into a line of vehicles or driving much too close to the vehicle in front, especially when the purpose is to cause the other vehicle to pull to one side to allow the accused to overtake
- disregard of traffic lights and other road signs, which, on an objective analysis, would appear to be deliberate
- failure to pay proper attention, amounting to something significantly more than a momentary lapse
- overtaking which could not have been carried out with safety
- driving with a load which presents a danger to other road users.

CARELESS DRIVING

The offence of driving a mechanically propelled vehicle on a road or other public place without due care and attention contrary to section 3 Road Traffic Act 1988 is a summary only offence. For the meanings of 'mechanically propelled vehicle', 'road' and 'public place' see *Chapter 1*.

What is careless driving?

The statutory provision itself is silent as to the nature of careless driving, this being something for courts themselves to determine. The decided cases show that the offence is committed when the driving falls below the standard expected of a reasonable, competent and prudent driver, in all the circumstances. The following are examples of driving which may support an allegation of careless driving, as agreed by the Police and Crown Prosecution Service:

- overtaking on the inside
- driving inappropriately close to another vehicle
- driving through a red light
- emerging from a side road into the path of another vehicle
- turning into a minor road and colliding with a pedestrian.

The above all involve more than momentary inattention and the safety of other road users is affected. Other examples of driving which may support an allegation of careless driving include situations where the driver's conduct clearly caused him or her not to be in a position to respond in the event of an emergency on the road such as:

- using a hand-held mobile telephone while the vehicle is moving (see *Appendix D* to this handbook), especially at speed
- tuning a car radio
- reading a newspaper or map
- selecting and lighting a cigarette/cigar/pipe
- talking to and looking at a passenger which causes a driver more than momentary inattention
- leg and/or arm in plaster
- fatigue/'nodding off'.

Penalty for careless driving
Careless driving is a summary only offence carrying a Level 4 fine (i.e. maximum £2,500) *discretionary* disqualification for any period and/or until a driving test has been passed. The power to disqualify until a driving test has been taken should be considered where there is reason to think that the driver is lacking in competence to drive. The court must endorse the driver's licence with 3 to 9 penalty points unless there are special reasons not to do so (see *Chapter 7*).

Careless driving: some general considerations
Sometimes the facts speak for themselves—a driver from a side road emerges into the main road, there is a collision and the driver from the side road cannot explain his or her manoeuvre. In these circumstances the court may have no option but to convict. In a case in 1993, the driver of a box van collided with the rear of a stationary vehicle, shunting it into the rear of another vehicle which was also stationary and waiting to turn right. Extensive damage was caused to both the front and rear of the middle vehicle and damage was also caused to the front of the

defendant's vehicle and to the rear of the first vehicle. The defendant had been driving along a clear road with no vehicles in front of him. His speed at the point of impact was 15 to 20 mph. The justices acquitted, holding that the prosecution had failed to establish the cause of the accident. In the High Court it was stated that there was nothing in the weather or road conditions which could explain the accident; there was no possible explanation for the collision other than the defendant was driving without due care and attention and no reasonable tribunal could find the defendant 'not guilty': *Director of Public Prosecutions v. Cox,* Queens Bench Division, January 1993. However, if there is a reasonable explanation it will then be for the prosecution to disprove this, and its failure to do so may enable the defendant to benefit from there being a reasonable doubt.

In dealing with allegations of driving without due care and attention, the issue for the court in considering sentence is the quality of driving and not its consequences. This was held to be so by the Court of Appeal in a 1995 case where three people had been killed. That court indicated that only the degree of carelessness and culpability should be considered by the sentencing court and not the unforeseen and unexpected consequences of the careless driving. In considering the issue of guilt, *The Highway Code* may often be helpful.

From time to time, courts will have to consider whether a mechanical defect was a factor in the alleged bad driving. An unknown mechanical defect may afford a defence, provided it could not reasonably have been foreseen.

Automatism may be a defence to an allegation of driving without due care and attention. Automatism is the involuntary movement of a person's body or limbs and is largely a matter of law: 🕮✋. The defence of automatism will not apply if the driver knew he or she had an illness likely to affect control of the vehicle.

In *R v. Backshall, The Times,* 30 March 1998 it was held that the defence of 'necessity' or 'duress of circumstance' can apply in relation to the offence of careless driving.

WITHOUT REASONABLE CONSIDERATION

There is a distinction between driving without reasonable consideration for other road users and driving without due care and attention, albeit both fall under the same provision of the Road Traffic Act 1988, i.e. section 3. If someone is prosecuted for *both* offences he or she can allege duplicity and ask the prosecutor to opt for one or other charge: 🕮✋

The offence of driving without reasonable consideration is committed if a person drives a mechanically propelled vehicle on a road or other public place without reasonable consideration for other persons using the road or place. For the meaning of such terms as 'mechanically propelled vehicle', 'road' and 'public place', see *Chapter 1*. It is a summary only offence and carries the same penalties as driving without due care and attention (above). The main difference between this offence and driving without due care and attention is that the prosecutor, in relation to this offence, must produce evidence that some other user of the road or public place was actually inconvenienced. Accordingly, a prosecution based upon the normal (or potential) traffic conditions for a road or public place will not succeed. For there to be a successful prosecution there must be evidence of actual inconvenience rather than the potential for such inconvenience. The following are examples of what might be sufficient bad driving to merit prosecution:

- driving with undipped headlights which dazzle oncoming drivers
- cutting in front of another vehicle at a roundabout
- failure to observe lane discipline
- unnecessary slow driving or breaking without good cause
- flashing of lights to force other drivers in front to give way.

All that needs to be shown is that the driver inconvenienced another road user—hence the conviction does not depend on the standard of driving.Other users include cyclists, pedestrians and even passengers in the same vehicle. In one case, a bus driver was successfully prosecuted because of the manner in which he drove his double decker bus, and the affect it had on the passengers in the bus at the time.

ALTERNATIVE VERDICTS

Normally, when magistrates acquit someone they are unable to convict for a lesser offence (unless the defendant also been charged with such lesser offence and the two matters are being tried together). However, someone whom they acquit of dangerous driving may be convicted of a lesser offence of careless or inconsiderate driving, despite the fact that he or she has not been charged with the lesser offence.

Causing death by careless driving when under the influence of drink or drugs

This offence was introduced when the Road Traffic Act 1991 inserted a new section 3A into the Road Traffic Act 1988. It is triable only on indictment and carries a maximum penalty of ten years imprisonment and/or an unlimited fine. There is also an obligatory disqualification for a minimum of two years, unless special reasons apply (*Chapter 8*).

The offence is committed if someone causes the death of another person by driving a mechanically propelled vehicle on a road or other public place without due care and attention or without reasonable consideration for other persons using that road or public place, and the driver is at the time of driving unfit to drive through drink or drugs; or has consumed so much alcohol that the proportion of it in the blood, breath or urine at that time exceeds the relevant prescribed limit; or is, within 18 hours after that time, required to provide a specimen but, without reasonable excuse, fails to do so. There must also be a clear causal link between the driving and the death.

What has been said earlier about the terms 'mechanically propelled vehicle', 'road' and 'public place' (see *Chapter 1*) applies here also.

'BAD DRIVING' AND SIMILAR OFFENCES

There are a number of other offences of a similar type to dangerous and careless driving, but which cater for specific circumstances.

Motor racing

This is a purely summary offence with a maximum penalty of a Level 4 fine, i.e. £2,500.

Conviction carries a mandatory disqualification for a minimum of 12 months in the absence of special reasons (see *Chapter 8*). The criteria for the offence is the promotion of or the taking part in a race or trial involving at least two vehicles on a public highway without the authorisation of the secretary of state.

Driver injuring persons by wanton or furious driving

This is an offence which may only be dealt with at the Crown Court, unless committed by a youth.

It carries a maximum sentence on conviction of two years imprisonment and/or an unlimited fine. The offence relates to the use of mechanically propelled vehicles, cycles and other carriages.

It must be shown that the offender was in charge of a carriage or vehicle and by wanton driving or racing or by other conduct did, or caused to be done, any bodily harm to any person. Accordingly, riding a cycle on private land could result in this offence being charged.

A conviction for this offence will not result in endorsement or disqualification.

Causing danger to road users

The Road Traffic Act 1991 introduced this new offence by virtue of adding a new section 22A to the Road Traffic Act 1988. The reason for the introduction of the offence was the difficulties and dangers caused to road users by obstructions put or thrown onto roads which either hit vehicles or with which vehicles then collided.

The offence is wider than mere interference with motor vehicles. It is committed if a person intentionally and without lawful authority or reasonable cause

- causes anything to be on or over a road; or
- interferes with a motor vehicle, trailer or cycle; or
- interferes (directly or indirectly) with traffic equipment in such circumstances

such that it would be obvious to a reasonable person that to do so would be dangerous.

The definition of 'traffic equipment' is very wide and, *inter alia,* includes: anything lawfully placed on or near a road by a traffic authority, or a lawfully placed road sign, fence, barrier or light. An example of the offence might be where a person intentionally interferes with temporary traffic lights or deliberately places nails on roads.

The offence can only be committed *intentionally,* and is an either-way offence. On indictment, it carries a maximum penalty of seven years imprisonment or an unlimited fine or both. On summary conviction, it carries at maximum six months imprisonment and/or a Level 5 fine (i.e. £5,000 maximum). There must also be a clear causal link between the driving and the death. The offence does not carry endorsement or disqualification.

Not having proper control of a vehicle

This offence is mentioned, along with its varying levels of penalties for different classes of vehicles, in *Appendix D* to this handbook.

ACCIDENTS

The relevant legislation creates two separate offences, one or both of which may be capable of being committed according to the circumstances: 🕮 ✋

- failing to stop after an accident
- failing to report an accident.

Only certain accidents oblige a driver to stop or report them: those resulting either in personal injury to someone other than the driver or damage to another vehicle or trailer or to an animal or roadside property.

Wild animals are not included, e.g. squirrels, rabbits—nor does it include an animal *in* the vehicle or trailer which is being driven by the driver on whom responsibility falls. Dogs are included, but not cats.

Failing to stop after an accident

The offence occurs when owing to the presence of a mechanically propelled vehicle on a road an accident has occurred which falls within the above description, and the driver fails to stop—and when reasonably required to do so, fails: to give his or her name and address; the name and address of the owner of the vehicle (assuming it is not his or her own); and the registration number to a person having reasonable grounds for requiring this information. Accordingly, if the driver stops his or her vehicle but fails to give the details when asked, say, by the driver of another vehicle with which there has been a collision the offence is committed. Equally, when the driver stops and walks away, the offence is likely to be made out, even if he or she returns later. However, everything depends on the circumstances, including the reason for departure, cause of failure and the length of the delay.

In relation to both this offence and the offence of failing to report the accident, lack of fault in relation to the accident on the part of the driver is no defence. Often there will be a duty on drivers to exchange information, whoever may be at fault.

The obligation to stop and give one's name and address only occurs if the driver knows of the accident or ought reasonably to have known of it. The prosecutor may bring evidence of this knowledge such as the fact that there was a loud bang or that the vehicle in question 'jolted', to prove the damage or injury. However, once the damage or injury is proved, it is for the defendant to prove lack of knowledge on a balance of probabilities.

Where there has been an accident, the driver should remain at the scene as long as is appropriate in the circumstances. Different considerations may apply, depending on the time of day and night and the area in question and whether the other vehicle was empty and so on. There will still be an obligation to report the accident (below).

Failing to report an accident

This offence occurs where the driver of a mechanically propelled vehicle, owing to the presence of which on a road an accident (which falls within the above description) occurs, has *not* given his or her name and address and that of the owner (if different) together with the registration number of the vehicles as outlined above, if he or she then fails to report the accident to a constable as soon as reasonably practicable or in any case within 24 hours thereof.

If a driver *has* stopped after an accident and given the prescribed particulars, there is no obligation to report it to the police.

Insurance

Where there has been personal injury to another person following an accident, then if the driver does not at the time produce a certificate of insurance to a constable or to some other person who has reasonable grounds for requiring him or her to produce it, there is an obligation on the driver to report the accident *and* produce a certificate of insurance at a police station or to a constable as soon as is reasonably practicable and in any case within 24 hours of the accident. If the certificate of insurance cannot be produced at the time of reporting, the certificate must be produced within five days.

Nature of the reporting

Any report to a police station must be *in person*, and a telephone call will not suffice. It should be noted that someone who reports after an unreasonable delay (albeit within 24 hours) may still, technically speaking, commit the offence of failing to report. Again, everything depends on the precise circumstances. The question for the court is 'Did the defendant report the accident "as soon as reasonably practicable"?'

Other considerations

The term 'injury' in relation to an accident may even include an hysterical or nervous condition. The type of other vehicle being damaged is not limited to motor vehicles and could include barrows, bicycles and horse drawn carts.

If a driver *was* unaware of an accident and subsequently realises what must have happened (for example, someone informs him or he notices damage to his or her vehicle) then he or she is still under an obligation to report within the 24 hour period—albeit that there may be a defence to an allegation of failing to stop.

Penalty

Parliament has recognised the seriousness of 'hit and run' driving in making both failing to stop after an accident and failing to report an accident imprisonable offences. It is perhaps no coincidence that in practice the offence is often committed late at night where there is also evidence of drinking. Other aggravating factors may include: the offence being committed whilst on bail; serious injury; a failure to remain at the scene; previous convictions and failure to respond to previous sentences, if relevant. Mitigating factors might include staying at the scene but not providing the full particulars through mistake or the fact that there was only very minor, possibly debatable damage.

The maximum penalty both for failing to stop or for failing to report is a Level 5 fine (i.e. maximum £5,000) and/or six months imprisonment. The offender's licence must be endorsed with 5 to 10 penalty points. As with all endorsable offences, disqualification is discretionary: *Chapter 8*. Guidance to the courts suggests that the driver should be disqualified if the offence can be regarded as serious.

The offence of failing to produce insurance carries a maximum fine of Level 3 (i.e. £1,000). It is both a non-imprisonable and non-endorsable offence: *Chapter 4*.

Compensation for road accidents

In most cases, compensation arising from road traffic accidents will not be ordered through the magistrates' court. However, an order can be made in respect of personal injury, loss or damage (other than that suffered by dependents as a result of death) due to an accident arising out of the presence of a mechanically propelled vehicle on a road in certain circumstances. These—and also civil remedies—are discussed in *Chapter 9*.

CHAPTER 3

Offences Involving Drink and Drugs

The breathalyser and its associated alcohol-related testing procedures were first introduced into England and Wales in 1967 by the Road Safety Act of that year. The intention was that the new law would be an effective deterrent to drinking and driving, and straightforward in operation. But the provisions proved complex and technical—and tended to invite legal challenge. In 1976, the Blennerhasstet Report suggested changes and these have been incorporated into what is now the Road Traffic Act 1988 (as amended), relevant parts of which form the main subject matter of this chapter. In the green paper *Combatting Drink Driving: Next Steps* (February 1998) the government suggests reducing the blood alcohol limit and introducing a sliding scale of penalties.

Quite apart from the specific offences described in this chapter, the presence of alcohol or drugs in the body of a driver will often be an aggravating factor in relation to other road traffic offences: see *Chapter 2* under *Dangerous Driving* and, generally, *Chapter 9*. In one instance drink/drugs aggravate the definition of the offence itself: see *Causing death by careless driving when under the influence of drink or drugs* in *Chapter 2*.

SUMMARY OF OFFENCES

This chapter describes motoring offences involving drink and drugs where this is the principle feature of the offence. In summary:

- *Failing to supply a roadside specimen* (section 6(4) RTA 1988) This offence is committed if someone fails to provide a specimen of breath for a breath test when required to do so by a police officer (by means of what is sometimes described as a 'hand held device' to distinguish it from the breath analysis machine at a police station: discussed later). Failure includes a refusal. Whether a constable may require a motorist to provide a preliminary breath sample depends upon whether the officer suspected the person concerned of committing a moving traffic offence or of having alcohol in his or her body, or whether the person has been involved in a traffic accident. The provisions are wide enough to encompass not only motorists who are or were *driving* but also those who are or were *in charge* of a motor vehicle. The constable's suspicion does not have to arise whilst the motorist is still driving or attempting to drive and he or she may require a breath test in respect of someone who has been driving.

- *Driving or attempting to drive a vehicle while unfit through drink or drugs* (section 4(1) RTA 1988) It is an offence for someone to *drive or attempt to drive* a vehicle on a road or in some other public place while unfit through drink or drugs. This offence does not involve the breathalyser, but can be charged where the prosecutor relies on other evidence of drink or drugs. Nowadays, it is particularly apposite in relation to drugs, where, as yet, there is no equivalent of the breathalyser. Voluntary testing of a new method of 'instant' drug detection are currently taking place and a good deal of publicity has attached to these experiments.

- *Being in charge of a vehicle while unfit through drink or drugs* (section 4(2) RTA 1988) It is an offence for someone to be *in charge* of a vehicle on a road or other public place while unfit through drink or drugs. It is a defence for the alleged offender to prove that there is no likelihood of his or her driving while unfit.

- *Driving or attempting to drive a motor vehicle 'with excess alcohol' in the blood, breath or urine* (section 5(1)(A) RTA 1988) It is an offence for someone to *drive or attempt to drive* a motor vehicle on a road or other public place with excess alcohol (i.e. beyond the prescribed limit) in his or her breath, blood or urine as evidenced by a certificate of analysis or a printout from an approved breath testing device. In practice this means the Lion Intoximeter (or less frequently the Camic Breath Analyser) although a new generation of analyser is being introduced: see under *New breath testing device* later in this chapter. It is not usually a defence that a defendant was not arrested or validly arrested. However, there may be a defence if the level of alcohol is due to consumption of alcohol *after* the offence. A *bona fide* claim of duress can also be a defence.

- *Being in charge of a motor vehicle with 'excess alcohol' in the breath, blood or urine* (section 5(1)(B) RTA 1988) It is an offence for someone to be *in charge* of a motor vehicle on a road or other public place with excess alcohol (i.e. beyond the prescribed limit) in his or her breath, blood or urine. It is a defence for the alleged offender to prove that there was no likelihood of his or her driving the vehicle whilst over the limit.

- *Failing to provide a specimen for analysis* (section 7(6) RTA 1988) Where someone is over the limit, they can be required to provide a specimen of breath, blood or urine for analysis (the kind of specimen depending on rules discussed later). It is an offence for someone who has been required to provide such a specimen to fail without reasonable excuse to do so.

In relation to the above offences, the offender is liable to compulsory disqualification if he or she was *driving or attempting to drive.* Where he or she was *in charge,* the offence is endorsable and attracts ten penalty points and discretionary disqualification.

THE ROADSIDE BREATH TEST

As the law stands, the police have no authority to administer random breath tests. The power to breathalyse a motorist only arises in two distinct sets of circumstances, i.e. 'upon suspicion' or where an accident has occurred.

Power to demand a specimen of breath 'upon suspicion'
A constable in uniform may require a breath test where he or she has *reasonable cause to suspect* one of the following:

- that someone *driving, attempting to drive or in charge* of a motor vehicle on a road either
  —has alcohol in his or her body: or
  —has committed a traffic offence whilst the vehicle is in motion
- that the person *has been* driving or attempting to drive or *has been* in charge with alcohol in his or her body and he or she still has alcohol in his or her body
- that the person *has been* driving or attempting to drive or *has been* in charge and has committed a traffic offence whilst the vehicle was in motion.

Constable in uniform
The power to require a roadside specimen may only be exercised by a constable in uniform. The term 'constable' refers to any member of a police force (i.e. not to the rank of the officer). It is a question of fact whether the officer is in uniform, but he or she must be identifiable as a police officer.

May require
No set form of words is required. It is sufficient if the language used can be fairly said to be capable of amounting to a requirement, e.g. 'I intend to give you a breath test'.

Reasonable cause to suspect

There is no need to prove that alcohol has been consumed or that a traffic offence has been committed, merely that the police officer *suspects* it on *reasonable grounds.* The suspicion does not have to be based upon first-hand observation, provided that it is reasonable. Thus, e.g. one officer can act upon information supplied by another, or, in appropriate circumstances, upon information supplied by a member of the public.

Moving traffic offence

The offence must have been a *moving traffic offence* committed under one of the following enactments:

- Public Passenger Vehicles Act 1981 (Part II)
- Road Traffic Regulation Act 1984
- Road Traffic Offenders Act 1988 (RTOA 1988)
- Road Traffic Act 1988 (RTA 1988)
- Road Traffic Act 1991 (RTA 1991)

Driving or attempting to drive or in charge

Whether someone is driving or attempting to drive or in charge is a question of fact. There are rulings of the higher courts which indicate that the vehicle does not have to be in motion and that a motorist can still be driving for a short time after ceasing to drive. As already indicated, section 6(1) RTA 1988 allows a constable to require a breath test not only from someone who *is* driving or attempting to drive but also from a motorist who *has been* driving or attempting to drive or *has been* in charge of a motor vehicle.

At or near the place where the requirement is made

By section 6(3) a test must be administered at or near the place where the requirement is made, but not necessarily exactly where the suspected offence (or accident: below) occurred. This has been held to be a matter of fact or degree. In one case 1.5 miles and in another 160 yards was held to be not 'there or nearby'.

Power to require a breath test following an accident

A police officer can require a breath test if an accident occurs owing to the presence of a motor vehicle on a road or in some other public place (section 6(2)).

As already indicated, the request can be made to anyone who the constable has reasonable cause to suspect of driving or attempting to drive, or who is or was in charge of the vehicle at the time of the accident. The request *can,* where the circumstances so dictate, be made some hours later.

Accident

It was held in *R v. Morris* [1972] RTR 201 that an accident was 'an unintended occurrence which had an adverse physical result'. It now appears that the test is whether an ordinary man would conclude on the facts that there had been an accident: see the definition in *Chapter 1.*

It is not essential that another vehicle was involved. The power to breathalyse after an accident extends to people who are merely believed by the officer to have been driving or in charge of the vehicle at the time of the accident. Subject to what is said about people in hospital (see under next sub-heading), the requirement can then be made automatically: i.e. there is no need for the officer to suspect consumption of alcohol, or to be in uniform.

Hospital patients

Section 9 RTA 1988 provides that if someone is at a hospital *as a patient* he or she cannot be required to provide a breath test or specimen for analysis until the medical practitioner in immediate charge of the case has first been notified of the proposal to require a breath test and does not object. A suspect has been held to be 'at a hospital' if anywhere within the precincts of the hospital (e.g. the hospital car park).

Powers of entry

In *Fox v. Chief Constable of Gwent* [1984] RTR 402 it was held that where the police were trespassers and administered a breath test, the conviction of the defendant for refusing the preliminary breath test should be quashed. However, a conviction under section 5 RTA 1988 of the defendant, who had supplied specimens of breath at the police station on the Lion Intoximeter, was upheld. It is only where the evidence of the Intoximeter is obtained by a trick, oppression or improper inducement that it is possible for the evidence of the printout to be excluded. The fact that the initial arrest was unlawful does not normally have this effect: 🕮✋

DRIVING OR IN CHARGE WHILST UNFIT

Under section 4(5) RTA 1988 a person is to be regarded as 'unfit to drive' if his or her ability to drive properly is *for the time being impaired.*

Impairment might, e.g. be proved by evidence that a car was being driven erratically or that the driver was involved in an accident at a spot where there is no hazard for a normal driver.

There will also need to be evidence of drink or drugs, but this can be provided by any admissible means. There might, e.g. be evidence of inability to stand, incoherence, slurred speech, mental confusion or the smell of alcohol and no other explanation for the defendant's condition (some medical conditions or personal traits can simulate alcohol or drug impairment when medical evidence may become necessary).

Drug is defined as including 'any intoxicant other than alcohol' (section 11). The drug does not have to be an illegal drug: driving when unfit due to prescribed medication is just as unlawful as driving when suffering from the effects of, say, marijuana.

Section 4(6) allows a constable to arrest someone without warrant if he or she has reasonable cause to suspect that that person is or has been committing an offence under these provisions.

DRIVING OR IN CHARGE ABOVE THE LIMIT

For the purposes of an offence of 'excess alcohol' contrary to section 5(1)(A), the meaning of 'consuming' is not limited to drinking. It could, e.g. include an injection of alcohol. The offence requires the offender to be driving or attempting to drive a motor vehicle on a road or public place. The prescribed limit is:

35 micrograms of alcohol in 100 millilitres of breath
80 milligrams of alcohol in 100 millilitres of blood
107 milligrams of alcohol in 100 millilitres of urine

Analysis of blood or urine specimens must be made by an authorised analyst.

Challenging the analysis

The defendant can seek to challenge the analysis by proving that the sample he or she was given at the police station produced a significantly different analysis, or that he or she had consumed alcohol *after* the commission of the offence but before the sample was taken (see *Post offence consumption* below).

Provision of specimens at a police station

Only certain police officers have been trained to operate the Lion Intoximeter (the regular evidential breath testing machine in England and Wales) and it can only be operated by such an individual.

Breath specimens

A motorist may be required to provide *breath* specimens for analysis at a police station, i.e. by the Intoximeter.

Blood or urine specimens

There are four situations in which the police can ask *for blood or urine* specimens:

(i) where the constable making the requirement has reasonable cause to believe that for medical reasons a specimen of breath cannot be provided or should not be required.

(ii) where at the time the requirement is made a device or reliable device (the Lion Intoximeter or Camic Breath Analyser) is not available at the police station or it is for any other reason not practicable to use one.

(iii) where the suspected offence is one under section 4 RTA 1988 (driving or in charge whilst unfit through drink or drugs) and the constable making the requirement has been advised by a medical practitioner that the condition of the person required to provide the specimen might be due to some drug.

(iv) where an approved device has been used at the police station but the constable who required the specimens of breath has reasonable cause to believe that it has not produced a reliable indication of the proportion of alcohol in the breath of the person concerned.

With regard to (i) it is for the police officer to decide whether there is a valid medical reason but he may seek professional help. The machine does take a considerable amount of breath at a required pressure.

In (ii) if the calibration check of the machine is not within prescribed levels or if the machine does not satisfactorily purge itself it would seem a reliable device is not available. High Court rulings indicate that someone can be taken to another police station to use a similar device or for a blood sample.

(iv) is intended to cover the situation where using more modern equipment the officer will know if the machine is malfunctioning.

Defendant's option to provide blood or urine specimens

If the lower of the two breath specimens is no more than 50 micrograms the defendant may claim that it be replaced by blood or urine. The defendant cannot choose which—it is for the constable to decide which sample should be taken. There have been a number of rulings with regard to this option and it is clear that the defendant will be entitled to be acquitted if he or she:

- is not told of this option
- is mistakenly required to provide a blood sample

- exercises the option and through no fault on his or her part the blood (or presumably urine) sample cannot be used
- is not given the option of providing urine when he or she might have a medical reason for not providing a blood sample
- has improper pressure exerted on him or her not to exercise the option to provide a specimen for laboratory analysis.

It was stated in *Director of Public Prosecutions v. Warren* [1992] 4 All ER 1865 that when making a decision as to whether the specimen should be blood or urine the police officer does not have to invite the driver to express his or her own preference before making that decision.

BACK CALCULATION

By the defence

By section 15(2) RTOA 1988 a court must assume that the proportion of alcohol in the defendant's breath, blood or urine at the time of the alleged offence was not less than that in the specimen. This is an irrebuttable presumption and backtracking is not permissible by the accused, even though it is possible for the prosecution.

By the prosecution

Section 5(1) RTA 1988 requires evidence that at the time of driving the defendant had excess alcohol in his breath or blood. This may be the case even though there is not excess alcohol in the breath etc. when the test is taken some time later. Medical evidence is admissible to prove that at the earlier time, when the defendant was driving or in charge, he or she was over the prescribed limit. This is done by way of back calculation on the basis of the amount of alcohol eliminated from the blood stream over a period of time. The calculation varies with the individual and depends on a combination of height, age, weight and physical condition.

In *Gumbley v. Cunningham* (1989) Crim. LR 297 when the test was taken 4 hours and 20 minutes after the accident there was a reading of 59 milligrams of alcohol in 100 millilitres of blood. Medical evidence indicated that a man of the defendant's type eliminated alcohol of between 10 and 25 milligrams per 100 millilitres per hour so that at the time of the accident there were about 120 to 130 milligrams per 100 millilitres of blood. He was convicted of driving with excess alcohol in the blood. In *Smith v. Gerahty* [1986] RTR 222, where a similar calculation was made, Lord Justice Glidewell said: 'Going back to the level of alcohol in the blood at the time of driving is clearly permissible but only practical . . . provided that there is reasonable clear straightforward and relatively simple evidence to show it . . . Justice ought not to be drawn into any detailed scientific calculations.' In practice, back calculation tends to be used quite sparingly.

As with all matters where the onus is on the prosecutor, if he or she seeks to rely on back calculation to prove that the defendant was above the prescribed limit, the relevant ingredients of the offence must be proved beyond reasonable doubt.

Evidential breath test devices

Section 7(1)(A) RTA 1988 requires the device to be of a type approved by the secretary of state. In order to avoid the police having to call evidence from someone on behalf of the Home Secretary, the Lion Intoximeter and Camic Breath Analyser have been approved by the Breath Analysis Devices (Approval) Order 1983. Either device may be used by any police force in England and Wales.

It is understood that the Lion Intoximeter is used by the great majority of police forces, the Camic Breath Analyser being used mainly in the North of England and Scotland. Both machines have a calibration check device consisting of a sealed jar containing a solution of alcohol at a given strength through which air is passed at a controlled temperature of 34 degrees centigrade which should produce a vapour at the prescribed limit, i.e. 35 micrograms.

Section 7(1)(A) requires the defendant to provide two specimens of breath on this device and section 8(1) that of the two specimens the one with the lower reading should be used and the other disregarded. Where the alcohol levels for the two specimens are the same, either may be used.

Challenging the reliability of the Intoximeter

Where the accuracy of the analysis is challenged on grounds of non-compliance with the instructions as to use, it would appear that the onus is on the defence to show that the instructions have not been complied with and that non-compliance is unduly favourable to the prosecutor. There have been numerous cases concerning the reliability or otherwise of the machine. In *Fawcett v. Gasparis* (1987) Crim. LR 53 failure to print the correct combination of day and date did not mean that the alcohol analysing function of the machine was unreliable. The House of Lords has upheld convictions in two cases where the clock, which showed the wrong time, did not affect the efficient operation of the computer producing the printout: *Director of Public Prosecutions v. McKeown; Director of Public Prosecutions v. Jones* [1997] 1 WLR 295.

Even if there is no printout at all the officer who operated the machine could give evidence of the readings on the visual display and that would be sufficient evidence for the court, unless there were other indications that the machine was unreliable. It would seem safer in this type of situation for the officer to avail himself of his right to require blood or urine instead.

One way in which the reliability of the device has been challenged has been by showing that the two successive breath samples differed from each other by more than 20 per cent. However in a case of *Maheraj v. Solomon* [1987] RTR 295 it was decided that in a case where the blow difference amounted to 20.9 per cent of the lower figure, but the machine was nevertheless demonstrated to be calibrating properly, magistrates were quite correct to convict (the breath samples revealed 81 and 67 micrograms respectively: both well above the prescribed limit). In *Lodge v. Chief Constable of Greater Manchester* (1988) Crim. LR 533 it was held that a disparity of 23.1 per cent (readings of 64 and 52 micrograms) did not compel a court to accept expert opinion that the machine was unreliable.

In *Cracknell v. Willis* [1987] 3 All ER 801 the House of Lords held that a motorist could not be prohibited from adducing evidence of the amount of alcohol he had consumed in order to show that the approved breath analysis device was defective. The presumption that the machine was reliable could be challenged and if challenged by relevant evidence (in that case it was said by calling two reliable witnesses—e.g. 'two bishops or judges'!— with whom the accused had dined to testify that he had drunk nothing alcoholic all evening) the justices would have to be satisfied that the machine had provided a reading upon which they could rely before making the assumption that it was working properly. In practice it is extremely difficult to challenge a breath analysis by evidence of lack of consumption of alcohol.

Blood specimens

Section 15(4) RTOA 1988 states that a specimen of blood must be taken from the accused with his or her consent by a doctor. It is for the doctor to say how the blood specimen should be taken and the defendant cannot demand that blood is taken from a particular part of the body.

The specimen of blood must be divided into two parts at the time it is provided and the part not sent to the police laboratory supplied to the defendant (section 15(5) RTOA 1988). Whilst the accused has to be given a part of the specimen of blood or urine if he or she asks for it, there is no obligation on the part of the police to remind him or her of this or to supply it in a suitable container. If section 15(5) is not complied with, the certificate is not admissible and the prosecution will fail. Where there is a discrepancy between the prosecutor's and defendant's sample—and thus a dispute—the court is entitled to prefer the prosecutor's analysis so long as the court is satisfied beyond reasonable doubt that the explanation it relies on is correct.

Certificate of analysis and printouts

Evidence of the proportion of alcohol or a drug in a specimen of breath, blood or urine, and that a specimen of blood was taken from the defendant with his or her consent by a medical practitioner, can be proved in proceedings for offences under sections 4 and 5 by the production in court of the following documents:

(i) a statement as to analysis of breath automatically provided by the Camic Breath Analyser or Lion Intoximeter with a certificate signed by the constable that the statement relates to a specimen provided by the accused at the date and time shown in the statement: see the example at page 56.

(ii) a statement signed by an authorised analyst as to the proportion of alcohol or any drug found in a specimen of blood or urine identified in the certificate; and

(iii) a certificate purporting to certify that a specimen of blood was taken from the accused with his or her consent by a medical practitioner purporting to be signed by a medical practitioner.

A copy of the breath test certificate of analysis must be handed to the defendant at the time it is created or not less than seven days before the hearing, otherwise it cannot be produced in evidence. Section 16(3) RTOA 1988 provides that other certificates (i.e. blood analysis) must be sent to the accused not later than 7 days before the hearing. In *Gaimster v. Marlow* [1984] RTR 49 it was held that a printout from a Lion Intoximeter is a statement within the meaning of section 123 RTOA 1988 and therefore admissible in evidence to prove the breath-alcohol level. In *Castle v. Cross* [1985] RTR 62 the printout was held admissible where it was alleged that the defendant had failed to provide a specimen. In *Reid v. Director of Public Prosecutions, The Times,* 6 March 1998 typographical errors in the printout did not invalidate the result of a properly calibrated and functioning machine. Justices should be slow to exclude evidence of the taking of the substantive specimen of breath because of a technical shortcoming in the roadside procedure: *Director of Public Prosecutions v. Kay, The Times,* 13 April 1998.

Post 'offence' consumption

In *Rowlands v. Hamilton* [1971] 1 All ER 1089 it was established that it is a defence to a charge of driving with excess alcohol that the accused had drunk alcohol after ceasing to drive and before the breath test was administered. Later cases have restricted the application of this rule and section 15(2) RTOA 1988 provides that it is for the accused to rebut the presumption that the alcohol in his or her breath was not less than that in the specimen. To do this he or she must prove two things:

- that he or she consumed alcohol after ceasing to drive the motor vehicle and before he or she provided the specimen; and
- that had he or she not done so the proportion of alcohol in his or her breath would not have exceeded the prescribed limit.

The burden of proof is upon the defendant although this will be discharged by proof on a balance of probabilities.

New breath testing device

A new breathalyser machine has been approved by the secretary of state. The Lion Intoxilyzer 6000 machine is being distributed to police forces in the United Kingdom and there is a rolling programme to replace all older models by the end of 1999. The new device uses state-of-the-art technology and it is hoped that it will eliminate challenges of the kind made to the reliability of evidence from its predecessors.

The procedure for conducting the test is similar to before but the new device produces a quicker result (2.5 minutes as opposed to 4 minutes). The manufacturers have expressed their confidence that there will be 'very little scope for challenge' to the machine in court.

Duress and insanity

The defence of duress may, in appropriate circumstances, be available in relation to an offence under section 5(1)(A) RTA 1988: 📖✋. In *Director of Public Prosecutions v. Bell* [1992] Crim. LR 176 it was indicated that duress may be established where fear engendered by threats causes someone to lose complete control of his or her will. In that case the defendant was chased to his car by people who were intent upon doing him harm. He drove off in panic and stopped when he thought he was safe. This was a significant factor. In *Director of Public Prosecutions v. Jones* [1990] RTR 33 duress was *not* a sustainable defence where the defendant had driven off to escape danger, but then drove all the way home. It was also indicated in these rulings that there has to be good cause to fear death or serious injury for this defence to be established.

In *Director of Public Prosecutions v. H, The Times,* 2 May 1997 it was held that insanity is not available as a defence, excess alcohol being an offence of strict liability.

IN CHARGE ABOVE LIMIT OR WHILST UNFIT

Whether or not someone is 'in charge' of a vehicle is a matter of fact and degree. In *Director of Public Prosecutions v. Watkins* [1989] 1 All ER 1126 the High Court provided guidance on the meaning of 'in charge'. That court indicated that whilst there could be no hard and fast all-embracing test, there were, broadly speaking two distinct classes of case:

- where the defendant was the owner or lawful possessor and had recently driven the vehicle. This person would normally be in charge and the question then arises whether he or she was still in charge or whether they had put the vehicle in someone else's charge. However, he or she would not be in charge if, in all the circumstances, they had ceased to be in actual contact and there was no realistic possibility of resuming actual control whilst unfit, e.g. where he or she was in bed at home for the evening or at some distance from the car or it had been taken by another individual.

- where the defendant was not the owner, lawful possessor or recent driver but was sitting in the vehicle or otherwise involved with it, the question would be whether he or she had assumed being in charge of the vehicle. They would be in charge if whilst unfit he or she was voluntarily in *de facto* control or might be expected imminently to assume control. The facts to be taken into account in making this decision would include:

  — whether and where he or she was in the vehicle or how far they were from it
  — what he or she was doing at the relevant time
  — whether he or she was in possession of a key that fitted the ignition
  — whether there was evidence of an intention to take or assume control of the car by driving or otherwise
  — whether any person was in, at or near the vehicle and, if so, the details of that person.

Statutory defences to 'in charge' allegations

Someone charged under section 4(2) with being in charge while unfit to drive through drink or drugs is deemed not to be in charge if he or she proves that at the material time the circumstances were such that there was no likelihood of his or her driving so long as he or she remained unfit to drive through drink or drugs. Similarly section 5(2) provides a defence to an offence of in charge in relation to excess alcohol if the defendant proves that at the time that he or she is alleged to have committed the offence the circumstances were such that there was no likelihood of his or her driving the vehicle whilst the proportion of alcohol in his or her breath, blood or urine remained likely to exceed the prescribed limit.

The onus of proof is upon the defendant—on a balance of probabilities. A highly material fact will be the level of alcohol recorded. Medical evidence would probably be needed to show when the defendant's alcohol level would decrease to the legal level, but other evidence such as arranging for someone else to drive or taking a bedroom at a hotel might also help to establish the special defence.

FAILING TO PROVIDE A SPECIMEN

Someone who without reasonable excuse fails to provide a specimen when required to do so pursuant to section 7 is guilty of an offence (section 7(6)).

A person can be lawfully required to provide specimens of blood, breath or urine in the course of an investigation whether that person has committed an offence under section 4 or 5. It is important to note that it is not necessary to prove a section 4 or 5 offence has been committed, but merely that there is a *bona fide* investigation.

Reasonable excuse

It is for the defendant to put forward a reasonable excuse, following which it is for the prosecutor to disprove its existence. Rulings of the High Court show that courts will not readily find the existence of a reasonable excuse. In particular, it has been held that an excuse cannot be judged reasonable unless the person from whom the specimen is required is physically or mentally unable to provide it or the provision of it would entail a substantial risk to his or her health: *R v. Leonard* [1973] RTR 252.

In *Alcock v. Reid* [1980] RTR 71 the accused did establish the defence when, being unable to provide a specimen of urine, he refused a request for blood on the grounds that he was mentally incapable of complying with the request as he had a terror of blood being taken from his body. A witness indicated he had blacked out on being a blood donor. It was held that this was evidence upon which the justices were entitled to infer that there was a reasonable excuse for refusing.

In *R v. Harling* [1976] RTR 441 the doctor made three unsuccessful attempts to obtain blood, so urine was requested. The defendant refused as he said he had lost all confidence in the doctor who was also going to test the urine. He was convicted because, although he had a good reason for refusing blood, there was no good reason for refusing urine.

The defendant would not appear to have a reasonable excuse simply because he wants to have his solicitor present *Law v. Stephens* [1971] RTR 358. Further, in *Director of Public Prosecutions v Billington* [1988] RTR 221 it was held that a refusal to give a breath specimen where the defendant had requested to see his lawyer under section 58 Police and Criminal Evidence Act 1984 (PACE) did not amount to a reasonable excuse.

A defendant who provides a first specimen of breath at the police station which shows that he is under the limit and then without reasonable excuse fails to provide the second specimen is guilty of an offence under section 7(6).

In *Cotgrove v. Conney* [1987] RTR 124 an acquittal under section 7(6) was upheld when the defendant, who the police accepted was co-operative and trying his best, failed to provide a breath specimen despite many attempts.

In *Grix v. Chief Constable of Kent* [1987] RTR 193 the police accepted that a specimen of breath could not be provided but requested blood. The defendant refused blood but offered urine. This was held not to be a reasonable excuse because the choice of alternative is for the police and not the accused.

In *Director of Public Prosecutions v Fountain* [1988] RTR 185 the defendant refused to give blood in view of the danger of aids. This was held not to be a reasonable excuse. However, in *De Freitas v. Director of Public Prosecutions* [1993] RTR 98 a man who was said to have a longstanding phobia of being injected with the aids virus did have a reasonable excuse. Magistrates faced with these and similar issues should take up to date advice concerning developments: 📖✋

PENALTIES AND OTHER ORDERS

The offences dealt with in this chapter are all triable summarily only. They are punishable as follows:

- *Failing or refusing to supply a roadside test* (section 6(4) RTA 1988) This offence is punishable with a maximum fine of £1,000. Endorsement is obligatory (4 penalty points) and disqualification discretionary.

- *Driving or attempting to drive a vehicle while unfit through drink or drugs* (section 4(1) RTA 1988) This offence is punishable with a maximum fine of £5,000 and or six months imprisonment. Endorsement is obligatory and a *minimum* disqualification of 12 months must be imposed in the absence of special reasons for not disqualifying. If the court does find special reasons the offence is punishable with 3-11 points and the court may still disqualify the defendant at its discretion.

- *In charge of a vehicle while unfit through drink or drugs* (section 4(2) RTA 1988) This offence is punishable with a maximum fine of £2,500 and/or three months imprisonment. Endorsement is obligatory with 10 penalty points and disqualification discretionary.

- *Driving or attempting to drive a motor vehicle with excess alcohol in the breath, blood or urine* (section 5(1)(A) RTA 1988) This offence is punishable with a maximum fine of £5,000 and/or six months imprisonment. Endorsement is obligatory and a minimum disqualification of 12 months must be imposed in the absence of special reasons for not disqualifying. If the court finds special reasons the offence is punishable with 3-1 l penalty points and the court may still disqualify the defendant at its discretion.

- *In charge of a motor vehicle with excess alcohol in the breath, blood or urine* (section 5(1)(B) RTA 1988) This offence is punishable with a fine of £2,500 and/or three months imprisonment. Endorsement is obligatory with 10 penalty points and disqualification is discretionary.

- *Failing to provide a specimen for analysis* (section 7(6) RTA 1988) When driving or attempting to drive, this offence is punishable with a fine of £5,000 and/or six months imprisonment. Endorsement is obligatory and a minimum disqualification of 12 months must be imposed in the absence of special reasons for not disqualifying. If the court finds special reasons the offence is punishable with 3-1 l points.

  When not driving or attempting to drive, the offence is punishable with a fine of £2,500 and/or three months imprisonment. Endorsement is obligatory with 10 penalty points and disqualification is discretionary.

Custody

A court can only impose a custodial sentence if the offence is so serious that only a custodial sentence can be justified for it (*Chapter 9*). In making this decision the court will need to consider all the circumstances of the case, the alcohol level and whether the offence is associated with an episode of bad driving. In *R v. Tupa* [1974] RTR 153 (confirmed more recently in the case of *R v. Shoult* [1996] RTR 298) it was declared that imprisonment for excess alcohol was appropriate where there was a high reading (i.e. over three times the legal limit).

Disqualification

Where obligatory disqualification is imposed the Magistrates Association guidelines recommend that the length of a ban should be related directly to the alcohol level of the offender: see *Appendix A* to this handbook. Therefore the higher the reading, the longer the disqualification will be.

Where a defendant is convicted of driving or attempting to drive whilst unfit (section 4(1)) or with excess alcohol (section 5(l)(A)) or refusing to supply a laboratory specimen (section 7(6)) when driving or attempting to drive at the relevant time and has been previously convicted of any such offence within a period of ten years, the minimum period for which a court is obliged to disqualify is increased to three years. A motorist who has been disqualified for the three year period may apply for removal of disqualification after two years.

In the case of 'high risk offenders' they will have to satisfy the DVLA that they do not have a drink problem before they receive their licence back. A high risk offender is an offender who fits the following criteria:

- someone disqualified for driving whilst 2.5 times or more over the prescribed limit
- someone disqualified for a second drink/drive offence within 10 years
- someone disqualified for refusing to supply a specimen for analysis.

Special reasons for not disqualifying

Where an order of disqualification from driving is obligatory, the relevant minimum period must be imposed unless special reasons are applicable. The underlying principles are discussed in *Chapter 8.*

Materials

A copy of a printout from the Lion Intoximeter appears overleaf. An example of a *Notification of Driving Disqualification* is reproduced on page 104.

Specimen Intoximeter Printout

Note that the sequence is as follows:

A first automatic calibration check (STD 34) is followed by a blank test of the sample chamber which is carried out by the machine automatically.

The first breath sample (23) is followed by a further automatic blank check of the machine. Similarly, the second breath sample (22) is followed by a further automatic blank test.

Finally, the machine carries out a second automatic calibration check (33).

UG% = micrograms of alcohol per 100 millilitres of breath: see page 44.

TEST RECORD

LION INTOX. 3000/3920
BLANKTOWN STATION
NUTSFORD POLICE 13HD

WED MAY 1ST 1998

SUBJECT NAME =
CAMBRIDGE AUSTIN
DOB = 130763

A. Cambridge

....
signature

TEST UG%	TIME
STD 34	20:45GMT
BLK 0	20:45GMT
ONE 23	20:46GMT
BLK 0	20:46GMT
TWO 22	20:47GMT
BLK 0	20:47GMT
STD 33	20:50GMT

OPERATORS NAME =
KENNY 1471

I CERTIFY THAT IN THIS STATEMENT, READING ONE RELATES TO THE FIRST SPECIMEN OF BREATH PROVIDED BY THE SUBJECT NAMED ABOVE; AND READING TWO TO THE SECOND, AT THE DATE AND TIME SHOWN HEREIN.

Sgt O J Kenny

....
Signature of Operator

CHAPTER 4

Legal Obligations and Documentation

Every motorist must hold a valid driving licence, be insured against third party risks, his or her vehicle must have a current vehicle excise licence (VEL) and must, if at least three years old, have a current Ministry of Transport (MOT) certificate. All these items are dealt with in this chapter which also looks at offences of fraud or dishonesty in relation to them.

INSURANCE

Section 143 Road Traffic Act 1988 requires every person who uses, causes or permits another to use a motor vehicle on a road to have a policy of insurance (or a security) in respect of third party risks in relation to use of the vehicle. Use of the motor vehicle without insurance is the most common insurance-related offence dealt with in magistrates' courts. Other offences commonly encountered are failure to produce insurance certificates and forgery or misuse of insurance certificates. Using, causing and permitting are explained in *Chapter 1*. Section 145 of the 1988 Act requires the policy to cover any liability that may be incurred in respect of the death of or bodily injury to any person, or damage to property caused by or arising out of the use of a vehicle on the road. Six limited exceptions are covered by section 145(3)(a): 📖✋

Under section 145, all authorised insurers are required to be members of the Motor Insurers Bureau (MIB). The MIB is established to provide compensation where the victim of a road traffic accident may be left without any other remedy. This will include where the responsible driver is uninsured, untraced or an insurance company has gone into liquidation. The relationship between the MIB and the requirement for courts to consider awarding compensation is dealt with in *Chapter 9*.

Certificate of insurance

Section 147 of the 1988 Act provides that a policy is of no effect unless and until the insurer delivers to the insured a certificate in the prescribed form. It is this certificate which defendants appearing at court will need in order to prove that they were covered.

The Motor Vehicles (Third Party Risks) Regulations 1972 (as subsequently amended) include amongst their provisions a power for the police to obtain a copy free of charge of the insurance certificate. It would appear that this is a little known, or certainly little used, provision in relation to proceedings in magistrates' courts. The onus is upon the defendant to produce a certificate once the prosecution have proved the relevant use of the vehicle. Defendants can and sometimes do encounter a good deal of difficulty in obtaining copy certificates and delays ensue. Whilst one can envisage arguments by the police against the use of the power to obtain copy certificates, delay would often be avoided if this provision was used regularly. In the event that a cover note has been issued, this is included in the definition of 'policy of insurance', and will provide satisfactory evidence of cover in the same way as a certificate.

A certificate (or cover note) is usually all that exists to prove that a policy of insurance is in existence. It is rare for the policy to be produced, since the certificate or cover note will usually deal adequately with all aspects of cover and in clearer, more concise terms.

The 'green card' is recognised in many countries as evidence that a motorist has insurance to cover the minimum requirements of that country. A valid green card is the equivalent of a policy of insurance. In the European Union a green card is not essential for British drivers, since their own insurance should contain cover for driving in EU countries.

Use

Various aspects of the use of vehicles in relation to insurance requirements have given rise to case law, covering such areas as the nature of the use (e.g. social, domestic and pleasure purposes; hire or reward), use by employees and agents, and use dependent upon the existence of a driving licence. Generally: 🕮✋

Car sharing

The extensive use of motor vehicles, particularly by single occupants is one of the causes of successive governments' views that efforts must be made to reduce congestion and thereby clean up the atmosphere. Most insurance policies exclude the use of the vehicle for hire or reward, whereas the sharing of cars by road users, particularly commuters should be encouraged. Section 150 Road Traffic Act 1988 provides that certain forms of car sharing must be covered by insurance policies. Restrictions include the fact that the vehicle must not be adapted to carry more than eight passengers, and must not be a motor cycle. In addition, the fare must not exceed the amount of the running costs of the vehicle for the journey. These conditions are set out in section 150(2).

Employees, etc.

With regard to employees and those classed as 'agents', a number of situations have been considered by the higher courts. Provided the driving by the employee is authorised, such use will normally be covered by the policy. Various aspects have been considered by the High Court, e.g. if someone leaves a car with a garage proprietor for work to be carried out, then the car owner is not employing the garage proprietor, and the proprietor cannot, therefore, rely upon the owner's cover: *Lyons v. May* [1948] 2 All ER 1062. In *Ballance v. Brown* (1955) Crim. L R 384, the question arose whether a defendant who had deviated from his normal route was still covered. On the particular facts of this case, the cover was held to be valid. It is clear, however, that the extent of the deviation from the norm will be a major factor.

Driver to be the holder of a licence

The requirement in a policy for the driver to be the holder of, or to have held, a driving licence is quite common. It is, however, important to check the precise wording of the condition, since certain of these are capable of wide interpretation. For example, if it is a condition that the driver, with the permission of the insured person, is one who 'holds or has held a driving licence' then this would include someone who had once held a licence, and such licence could even be provisional.

Similarly, driving disqualifications can give rise to disputes about cover. In *Adams v. Dunne* [1978] RTR 281, the defendant did not disclose the fact that he was disqualified when obtaining insurance, but the cover was held to be valid until declared void. Again, the importance of checking the precise wording of the policy becomes clear. A disqualified driver may still own a vehicle and allow it to be used by someone else, unless the driver has insurance cover he or she may be reliant upon the disqualified person's insurance. The wording of the particular insurance policy may well permit such use. Someone who is disqualified until a test is passed pursuant to section 36 Road Traffic Offenders Act 1988 (*Chapter 8*) is not apparently disqualified in the sense that this would render him or her uninsured, since he or she is allowed to apply for a provisional licence under section 37 of that Act, and thus continue to be a licence holder. Once again, the precise wording of the policy is important: 🕮✋

Unauthorised use and taking without consent

This is an offence under the Theft Act 1968: *Chapter 5*. Normally, unauthorised use will mean that such an offence has been committed (except where the defendant genuinely believes that he or she would have had that consent if the owner had known about the events). It is normally the case that the defendant guilty of taking a motor vehicle without consent is not covered by insurance. There are, however, exceptions, e.g. where the defendant has a policy covering *any* car. Many policies only cover driving with the permission of the vehicle owner. Again, the precise wording always merits attention:

Controlling or managing the vehicle
Under section 143 there must be an element of controlling, managing or operating the vehicle for it to be used. In *Thomas v. Hooper* [1986] RTR 1, the defendant was held not to be using a vehicle on tow when the steering was locked, there was no key, the brakes were seized, many parts needed replacing and the engine could not be started.

But this can be contrasted with the case of *Pumbien v. Vines* [1996] RTR 37 where a vehicle had been parked on a road whilst in working order and whilst covered by insurance. The certificate was thereafter cancelled, but in the meantime the condition of the vehicle had deteriorated significantly. It could not, for example, be moved without freeing the brakes, replacing the transmission pipe and oiling the gear box. It was nevertheless held to be a motor vehicle and in use.

A vehicle is in use on the road even when stationary and unattended, and must be insured, as stated in *Elliott v. Grey* [1959] 3 All ER 733 and *Adams v. Evans* [1971] CLY 10361.

Employers
An employer will normally be a user for the purposes of section 143 in addition to the employee driver. The same can be said of an owner who was with the driver. Likewise, passengers have been held to be using the vehicle when engaged in some joint enterprise with the person driving. An element of knowledge, however, in relation to passengers and their use of the vehicle without insurance must be present. Generally speaking, however, a passenger who is not the owner, and who merely sits by the driver, will normally commit no offence.

Employee's defence
Section 143 provides that an offence is committed by someone who uses, causes or permits an uninsured motor vehicle to be used on a road. The fact that the defendant in such circumstances did not know that it was uninsured is no defence. This is subject to the special defence provided by Section 143(3) of the 1988 Act for employees. The subsection provides a special defence for employees using vehicles in the course of their employment who did not know that the vehicle or the use of it was not covered. In *R v. Carr-Briant* [1943] 2 All ER 156 the burden of proof was said to rest with the defendant on the balance of probabilities. The employee must prove that the vehicle did not belong to him or her, that it was not in his or her possession under a contract of hiring or loan, that he or she was using the vehicle in the course of his or her employment,

and that he or she neither knew nor had reason to believe that the insurance was not in force.

Permitting

The offence of permitting the use of a vehicle without insurance is not committed by someone who allows a defendant to use the vehicle specifically on condition that the person is insured for its use. It must be emphasised that the fact that the permitter honestly believed that the vehicle was insured is no defence. It will only be a defence if this prior condition is insisted upon. There is a significant body of case law on the meaning of using, causing and permitting, and magistrates will need to seek advice in order to receive guidance on the various authorities: 🕮 ✋ (see also *Chapter 1*)

Burden of proof

Once the prosecution has shown that a vehicle was in use on a road and that no insurance certificate has been produced, the burden of proof switches to the defendant to show that the use was in fact covered by insurance. This burden of proof (on a preponderance of probabilities) will apply even though the user of the vehicle is not the owner. Difficulties in obtaining the necessary proof, e.g. the certificate, were discussed earlier in the chapter.

Section 165 Road Traffic Act 1988 allows the police to require the production of insurance certificates by drivers. As long as the certificate is produced within seven days of the requirement by that person, or anyone on behalf of that person, then no offence is committed. Production is to be at a named police station.

Production

It is a defence under section 165(4) to prove that the certificate was produced at the specified police station as soon as reasonably practicable, or it was not reasonably practicable for it to be produced at the specified police station before the day on which the proceedings were commenced. Proceedings are commenced when the information is laid. The onus of proving the defence rests on the defendant on the balance of probabilities.

Proceedings and penalties

An allegation under section 143 must be made by bringing proceedings within six months from the date on which the offence came to the knowledge of the prosecutor with an *overall time limit* of three years from the commission of the alleged offence. A certificate signed by or on behalf of the prosecutor indicating when evidence of the offence first came to his or her knowledge is conclusive evidence of that fact.

Offences under section 143 are summary only and attract a maximum fine of Level 5 (i.e. £5,000) and 6 to 8 penalty points. For special reasons for not endorsing see *Chapter 7* (and NB that a single conviction for no insurance will trigger the revocation provisions of the Road Traffic (New Drivers) Act 1998 which are discussed at the end of that chapter). Disqualification may be imposed for any period at the court's discretion or the offender may be disqualified until he or she passes a test.

The offence of failing to produce an insurance certificate is punishable with a maximum Level 3 fine (£1,000), and is triable only summarily. It is not an endorsable offence.

Motor Insurers Bureau

Reference was made earlier to the Motor Insurers Bureau (MIB). The requirement to award compensation is contained in section 35 Powers of Criminal Courts Act 1973: *Chapter 9.*

Where a driver is not insured, financial recompense can become a significant issue and it is important to note the interaction between the actions of the MIB and the compensation provisions. If the MIB is liable to meet a claim, then compensation cannot be ordered against an uninsured offender. The MIB will be liable for all injuries with certain limited exceptions (seek advice 🕮✋), but is not liable for the first £175 of property damage, nor for any property damage which exceeds £250,000 per accident. It follows, therefore, that in appropriate cases, it will not be unusual for courts to be asked to make an order for the first £175 of any property damage. The address of the MIB appears on page 117.

TEST CERTIFICATES (MOT)

Every motor vehicle first registered more than three years before the time when it is being used on a road must pass a test. Certain other vehicles, e.g. those used for carrying passengers, must be tested after one year. Many vehicles are exempt from the testing requirements, including tractors and agricultural vehicles. The regulations provide that vehicles are to be checked as to brakes, steering gear, certain lighting equipment and reflectors, stop lamps, tyres, seat belts and seat anchorages, direction indicators, windscreen wipers, washers, exhausts, horns, bodywork and the suspension of the vehicle. There are additional requirements for certain vehicles, e.g. concerning tachographs (see *Chapter 6*).

Test certificates are issued annually, but a vehicle re-tested in the last month of an existing certificate may have its new certificate expire on the anniversary of the expiry of the old one. The certificate can be issued by authorised examiners and certain other inspectors. These examiners are required to explain the grounds of refusal if a vehicle fails a test, and an appeal to the secretary of state is possible.

Use, cause or permit

An offence is committed if a vehicle is used, or caused or permitted to be used, without a test certificate. In summary, a vehicle is used not only when it is driven on a road, but when it is present on a road, even if it is not in roadworthy condition: see *Pumbien v. Vines* [1996] RTR 37. It has been said that the true test to be applied in the case of a stationary vehicle left on a road, is whether steps have been taken to make it impossible for the vehicle to be driven. Causing requires some express or positive authority from the person causing the vehicle to be used. It could also require some authority or knowledge of the facts constituting the offence. Permitting includes express permission, and also inferred permission. Using, causing or permitting are also mentioned in *Chapter 1*. Generally: 🕮✋

Production

A constable may require a driver or someone reasonably believed to be the driver, or someone reasonably believed to have committed a motor vehicle offence on a road, to produce a test certificate for inspection. It is an offence to fail to do so within a period of seven days. It is, however, a defence to say that the test certificate was produced at the specified police station as soon as is reasonably practicable or, if it is not reasonably practicable, for it to be produced at the specified police station before the day on which proceedings are commenced. The laying of an information commences proceedings. The burden of proof to establish the defences lies with the defendant, but the proof required is only on the balance of probabilities.

Goods vehicles

Goods vehicles are tested and plated by the Secretary of State for Transport at specified testing stations. Using such a vehicle on a road, or causing or permitting it to be used, without the necessary test certificate and/or plating certificate, are offences. The plated particulars required to be shown is a ministry plate, under the Construction and Use Regulations include details which identify the vehicle, its function, year of registration and manufacture, and various weight descriptions.

An authorised examiner may carry out a road side test of a motor vehicle, as to its brakes, silencer, steering gear, tyres, emission of smoke or fumes, lighting equipment, reflectors and noise. A constable may be an 'authorised examiner' for these purposes. Unless the constable considers that the vehicle is so defective that the test should be carried out forthwith, or that it has caused an accident, the driver may elect that the test be deferred.

Statutory defence
A vehicle need not have a test certificate if it is being used when proceeding to or from a test. The requirement is, however, for the test to have been 'by previous arrangement'. It is submitted that it is insufficient to fulfil the requirements of the defence to say that the garage advertised indicating that no prior notice was required.

Penalties
Using, or causing or permitting a vehicle to be used, without a test certificate is punishable by a fine on Level 3 (£1,000). The maximum penalty in respect of a vehicle adapted to carry more than eight passengers is a fine on Level 4 (£2,500).

Using, causing or permitting a goods vehicle to be used on a road without a test certificate carries a fine on Level 4, and use, etc., without a plating certificate, a fine on Level 3. An offence of failure to produce a certificate is punishable by a fine on Level 3.

None of these offences is imprisonable, and none carries endorsement of penalty points or disqualification. All are summary only offences.

DRIVING LICENCES

It is an offence for someone to drive on a road a motor vehicle of any class otherwise than in accordance with a licence authorising him or her to do so. To obtain a licence to drive unsupervised, a two stage test (theory and practical) must be passed. The theory test must be passed before the practical test can be taken.

The Road Traffic (New Drivers) Act 1995 provides that a driver who obtains six penalty points on his licence within two years of passing a first driving test, will lose his or her entitlement to drive otherwise than as a learner with a provisional licence—until he or she passes a further test (see *Chapter 7*). The court (or fixed penalty clerk: see *Chapter 9* under *A Note on Fixed Penalties*) must, when endorsing the licence, send it to the secretary of state for revocation. If an appeal is pending, the secretary of state must restore the entitlement to drive pending the outcome.

A full driving licence is issued until the holder attains the age of 70. After that age the licence is renewable every three years. An under-age driver may be prosecuted for driving otherwise than in accordance with a licence.

If an offender is disqualified until he or she passes a test of competence to drive (*Chapter 8*), he or she may immediately apply for a provisional licence and drive (subject to complying with its conditions, e.g. as to displaying L-plates and being accompanied by a qualified driver) once the application has been received.

An offence is committed by a licence holder who fails to surrender his or her licence forthwith when a change of name or address occurs.

Production

Production of licences to the court can be required under sections 7 and 27 Road Traffic Offenders Act 1988. Someone who fails to produce such a licence, or to send it to the court after the requirement has been imposed, commits an offence punishable by a fine on Level 3 (£1,000) unless he or she can satisfy the court that they have applied for a new licence and not received it. If someone drives after being required to produce a licence and failing to do so, he or she commits the offence of driving without a licence.

Section 164 of the 1988 Act allows the police to require production of driving licences. This power applies in respect of someone driving a motor vehicle on a road, or someone whom a constable or vehicle examiner has reasonable cause to believe was driving or was involved in an accident, or someone whom the constable or vehicle examiner has reasonable cause to believe has committed an offence on a road, and finally a person who is supervising a learner driver, or whom the constable or vehicle examiner reasonably believed was doing so when an accident occurred or an offence was suspected.

Once it is shown that a requirement to produce occurred, the onus is upon the defendant to show that the licence was produced, within seven days at the specified police station or as soon as is reasonably practicable, or if not reasonably practicable at the specified police station before the day on which proceedings are commenced (i.e. when the information was laid). Production of a driving licence at a specified police station is only effective if the defendant produces it in person. The defence is not available if it is produced by someone else on his or her behalf.

Cause or permit

It is an offence for someone to cause or permit another person to drive a motor vehicle on a road otherwise than in accordance with a licence. It is possible, therefore, for an employer to be prosecuted successfully under this provision. It appears that there is a valid defence open to an employer if the employee deliberately concealed the fact that he or she was unlicensed, i.e. knowledge is an essential ingredient as with aiding and abetting. Causing and permitting are also mentioned in *Chapter 1*.

Provisional licence

The offences of being a provisional licence holder and driving unsupervised and/or without L-plates have been abolished. The offence of driving *otherwise than in accordance with a valid licence* is sufficient to cover driving without a licence as well as the former offences of driving unsupervised and without L-plates. The onus is upon the prosecutor to prove that the vehicle was driven on a road, and thereafter it switches to the defendant to prove that he or she had a licence.

The supervisor in question must be genuinely supervising the driver, and seated in a position in the vehicle enabling proper supervision. A supervisor may be convicted of aiding and abetting offences such as careless driving. To be a qualified driver means that an appropriate licence must have been held *for at least three years,* and the person must be *at least 21 years of age.* This definition of 'qualified driver' appears in the Motor Vehicles (Driving Licences) Regulations 1996.

A provisional licence will last until the holder's seventieth birthday, with renewal every three years thereafter. Only one offence is committed by someone who fails to comply with the requirements of a provisional licence, namely that of driving otherwise than in accordance with the driving licence. The offence is endorsable and penalty points must be ordered in such circumstances: see *Penalties,* below.

A provisional licence holder: cannot carry a passenger on a solo motor cycle; must be accompanied by a qualified driver if driving a car.

Appeal

A right of appeal exists against refusal or revocation of a licence or a decision to grant a full licence for three years or less on the basis of physical fitness. A licence holder commits an offence if the physical fitness declaration in the application is one which he or she knew to be false. Section 22 Road Traffic Offenders Act 1988 places the court under a duty to notify the secretary of state where a defendant may suffer from a relevant disease or disability: see *Chapter 9* and seek advice as appropriate:

If at any time a licence holder becomes aware that he or she is suffering from a relevant or prospective disability, or that his condition has changed for the worse, they must notify the secretary of state accordingly. There is an exemption if the licence holder has not previously suffered from the condition, and reasonably believes that it will not last for more than three months.

There is a right of appeal to a magistrates' court against the refusal or revocation of a licence by the secretary of state.

Driver from abroad

A driver from abroad, who becomes resident in Great Britain, will be entitled to drive on his or her foreign permit in this country for a period of one year. This permit will entitle him or her to take a driving test within that year to obtain a full licence. At the end of one year, if he or she has not taken and passed a test, they must obtain a provisional licence. A disqualification imposed in England and Wales upon a UK citizen does not prevent use of an international driving permit abroad.

Penalties

Penalties for the most common summary only offences under this heading can briefly be described as follows:

- driving otherwise than in accordance with the licence, fine Level 3 (£1,000), endorsable with 3 to 6 penalty points if either no licence could have been granted, or the offender is under age, or no L-plates, unsupervised or carrying an unqualified passenger as appropriate
- causing or permitting a person to drive otherwise than in accordance with a driving licence carries of a fine on Level 3 but is *not* endorsable
- failure to produce a driving licence carries a fine on Level 3, but is *not* endorsable.

VEHICLE EXCISE LICENCES (VEL)

Vehicle excise duty is chargeable for every mechanically propelled vehicle which is being used or kept on a public road. The keeper is responsible for obtaining the relevant licence.

Mechanically propelled vehicle

The definition of what is, and is not, a 'mechanically propelled vehicle' has been the subject of much case law. The principal test is whether the vehicle has reached such a stage that it can be said that there is no reasonable prospect of it ever being made mobile again. Issues such as whether or not the vehicle still has an engine, and whether or not it might shortly be replaced, together with the general state of the vehicle—tyres deflated, brakes seized, gear box without oil and leaking transmission pipe, have all been debated. The onus of establishing that the vehicle is 'mechanically propelled' within the statutory provisions rests with the prosecutor. If such a point is raised, advice and a detailed analysis of the relevant authorities will be essential: 🕮 ☜ (see also the comments under *Definitions* in *Chapter 1*)

Use or keep

The other principal requirement of the offence is that the mechanically propelled vehicle was kept or used on a public road, that is to say one which is repairable at public expense, as defined in section 62(1) Vehicle Excise and Registration Act 1994. A vehicle will be *in use* when it is driven as well as when it is simply present on the road. A vehicle is being *kept* if it is caused to be on a public road when not in use.

Once the defendant is shown to have used or kept the vehicle on a public road, the burden of proving the purpose for which it was used rests with the defendant. The defendant must also show that it was licensed.

In order to attract duty, a mechanically propelled vehicle must be kept or used on a public road. The fact that the vehicle has not been driven, is not essential. A vehicle is kept on a road if it is caused to be there when not in use. *Ownership* is not essential to proof of *using* or *keeping*.

The position of an employed driver is that if the offence is committed whilst the vehicle is being used on the employer's business, then it is normally the employer and not the driver who should be summoned.

Exemptions

Section 5 Vehicle Excise and Registration Act 1994 provides certain exemptions from duty. The burden of proving that an exemption exists, rests with the defendant. Vehicles exempted from duty include:

- vehicles used on tram lines
- electrically assisted pedal cycles
- vehicles neither constructed nor adapted for use for the carriage of a driver or passenger
- vehicles used for police purposes
- fire-engines (whether kept by a public authority or other person)
- vehicles kept by a fire authority for the purpose of its fire brigade service
- ambulances for humans or animals.

Another notable exemption is that for vehicles being tested in an attempt to obtain an MOT test certificate (see earlier in this chapter) when proceeding to and from a previously arranged test, or where the test was failed, to and from the place where the relevant work is to be carried out on the vehicle by previous arrangement. The reference to previous arrangement, means that it must be specified as to time and date.

Penalties

Where an offence of using or keeping a vehicle on a public road without a licence is committed, the greater of the following penalties is provided as a maximum:

(a) an excise penalty on Level 3 (£1,000), or
(b) an excise penalty equivalent to five times the amount of duty chargeable and to back duty payment.

Proceedings for offences under section 29 of the Act must be commenced within six months of sufficient evidence coming to the knowledge of the prosecutor, with an overriding time limit of three years from the date of the offence. Prosecution can only be started by the Secretary of State for Transport or by a constable with approval.

Back duty

If someone is convicted of using or keeping an unlicensed vehicle, the court must order the keeper to pay, in addition to any penalty, back duty under sections 30 and 31 Vehicle Excise and Regulation Act 1994. The amount of back duty equates to one-twelfth of the annual rate of duty for each calendar month or part thereof, in the relevant period, which is defined by section 31 as:

- the period ending with the date of the offence and beginning:
  (a) if the defendant has before that date notified the licensing authority of his or her acquisition of the vehicle, with the date of receipt of that notification or, if later, with the expiry of the licence last in force for the vehicle; or
  (b) in any other case, the expiry of the licence last in force for the vehicle before the date of the offence or, if there has not at any time before that date been a licence in force for the vehicle, with the date on which the vehicle was first kept by that person.

Where the defendant is convicted and proves that throughout any month, or part thereof, the vehicle in question was not kept by him or her, or that he or she has paid the duty for the month or part thereof, no liability for back duty arises.

Vehicles 'off the road'

It is no longer the case—as it once was—that someone convicted of having no VEL is not liable for back duty by showing the vehicle was off the road, or that the vehicle was not kept or used by him or her on a public road, or even by showing that the vehicle was not chargeable with duty. Of course, back duty will only arise where the offence of using or keeping the vehicle without a licence is committed. If, therefore, a person takes a vehicle off the road so that no offence is committed to start with and it is untaxed, he or she will not be liable for any back duty if they licence the vehicle before putting it back on the road again.

It will, however, be possible to escape back duty if the defendant can show, on the balance of probabilities, that the vehicle was not kept by him or her but by someone else during the relevant period.

It should be noted that in connection with back duty, there *is no discretion* as to the amount. Unlike a fine, there is no power or requirement to take into account the defendant's means. Unless one of the exceptions under section 30 applies (see above), the full amount must be ordered. Furthermore, neither the excise penalty nor the back duty falls within the strict definition of a 'fine' in the Magistrates' Courts Act 1980 and, therefore, neither is capable of being remitted by a court inquiring into an offender's means at the default stage:

When disputing a back duty claim, the defendant should take the oath or affirm, and try to establish, e.g. that he or she was *not* the keeper at the relevant time or, as the case may be, that he or she has paid the duty for the relevant period or part thereof.

It should be noted that there is now a scheme of 'Statutory Off Road Notification' (SORN) which was introduced in order to produce accuracy of DVLA records and reduce duty evasion. As a result, the keeper of a vehicle which becomes unlicensed is required to provide a declaration to the DVLA. The DVLA is encouraging compliance with the requirement and undertaking a publicity campaign. It states that 'Enforcement action will begin when the Agency is content that the public understand the new procedures' (DVLA Circular, 9 February 1998). Other provisions cover the situation where a keeper gives a SORN notice but then takes the vehicle out on the road:

Failure to exhibit a VEL

Section 33 of the 1994 Act provides that it is an offence to fail to exhibit on a vehicle a licence in force for that vehicle. Whilst, technically, if there is no licence in force for the vehicle, the user may be prosecuted under section 29 for use without tax, and also for failing to display, it is not normal practice to proceed with both allegations. The penalty is a Level 1 fine (i.e. maximum of £200).

Strowger v. John [1974] RTR 124 is authority for saying that if the holder containing the licence falls from the windscreen onto the floor of the car and is no longer visible from outside, the offence of failing to exhibit a VEL is still committed. It is submitted that, other things being equal, this is a situation for an absolute discharge or at best a nominal penalty, if prosecuted in the first place.

Underpayment of duty

Section 37 of the 1994 Act deals with underpayment of duty. It provides that an offence is committed where a licence has been taken out for a vehicle at a particular rate, and the vehicle is used on a public road in such a way that a higher rate of duty becomes chargeable. The penalty is either a fine on Level 3 (£1,000) or an amount equal to five times the difference between the actual duty paid and the amount of duty at the higher rate. The time limit for proceedings under section 37 is six months from the date when evidence sufficient to justify the proceedings comes to the knowledge of the prosecutor, with an overall time limit of three years from the commission of the offence. Again, prosecution is only by the Secretary of State for Transport or by a constable with approval.

An order for payment of additional back duty is obligatory in respect of an offence under section 37. The amount is calculated on the basis of one-twelfth the difference between the relevant rates of duty payable for each month or part of the month in the relevant period.

Large goods vehicles (LGVs) and passenger carrying vehicles (PCVs)

A large goods vehicle is defined as a motor vehicle (not being a medium sized good vehicle within the meaning of Part III of the 1988 Act) which is constructed or adapted to carry or haul goods, and the permissible maximum weight of which exceeds 7.5 tonnes.

A passenger carrying vehicle means a large or a small passenger carrying vehicle as defined. A large passenger carrying vehicle is a vehicle used for carrying passengers constructed or adapted to carry more than 16 passengers. A small passenger carrying vehicle is a vehicle used for carrying passengers for hire or reward, which is constructed or adapted to carry more than 8 but not more than 16 passengers. It is an offence to drive on a road a motor vehicle of any class otherwise than in accordance with a driving licence authorising the driving of a motor vehicle of that class. Causing or permitting is also an offence. These offences will apply to people driving vehicles which require a particular large goods vehicle or passenger carrying vehicle licence. It is an offence to fail, without reasonable excuse, to comply with conditions of LGV or PCV licences, and the punishment is a Level 3 fine (£1,000).

Before LGV and PCV driving licences are authorised, the secretary of state must be satisfied, having regard to the conduct of the applicant, that he is a fit person to hold the licence. This conduct relates to the conduct as a driver in respect of the applicant for an LGV licence, and in respect of both driver and any other respect in relation to PCV licence.

If there is a failure or refusal to grant an LGV or PCV licence, the person aggrieved may appeal to a magistrates' court. Notice must first be given by the appellant to the secretary of state and any traffic commissioners to whom the matter has been referred. The procedure is by way of complaint to the magistrates' court acting for the area in which the appellant resides.

Penalties

Offences are summary only, non-imprisonable and punishable by a maximum Level 3 fine (£1,000). Only driving a class of vehicle other than in accordance with a licence for that class is endorsable with 3-6 penalty points and, therefore, attracts discretionary disqualification if either no licence could have been granted or provisional licence conditions were not complied with.

DISHONESTY INVOLVING DOCUMENTS ETC.

Although dishonesty in relation to obligations mentioned in this chapter or the falsification or misuse of documents may amount to a quite serious offence under the general law, special provision is made in certain situations.

Fraudulent use of excise licence

Section 44 Vehicle Excise and Registration Act 1994 provides that it is an offence for a person to fraudulently alter, use, lend or allow to be used a number plate, trade plate, vehicle or trade licence or registration document. This is an either way offence, punishable with a Level 5 fine (£5,000) if dealt with at the magistrates' court, or at the Crown Court with an unlimited fine or two years imprisonment, or both.

The root of the offence is avoidance of duty on a vehicle used on a public road. In *R v. Johnson* [1995] RTR 15 an altered vehicle excise licence on a vehicle parked on private land did not amount to fraudulent use of the licence. In *R v. Terry* [1984] RTR 129 it was held that the prosecutor did not have to prove an intent to avoid payment.

An offence of forging an appropriate licence or document can be prosecuted under section 44 of the Act, or indeed under section 1 of the Forgery and Counterfeiting Act 1981. 'Fraud' is defined in the 1981 Act.

Forgery etc. of documents

Under the Road Traffic Act 1988, there are several other offences involving forgery, alteration of documents and the making of false statements, for example to obtain a driving licence. Thus, in Section 173(1)(a) of that Act creates an offence of using with intent to deceive any documents referred to in that section. These include such documents as certificates of insurance, driving test certificates and the like. The more serious of these offences, such as forgery of a certificate of insurance, are either-way offences. Other offences such as making a false statement for the purposes of obtaining certain documents, e.g. a certificate of insurance, are summary offences. These provisions are complex and legal advice will is necessary: 🕮✋

CHAPTER 5

Theft, Taking Vehicles and Like Matters

As outlined in *Chapter 1* a distinction is sometimes drawn in practice between *criminal* offences and *road traffic* offences. In reality, the distinction is a false one, because both types of offence are criminal offences to which the same general principles, procedures and standards apply. Nonetheless, it is common for the distinction to be made, just as a similar one is made between 'criminal courts' and 'road traffic courts' in those areas of the country where work is separated out in this way. Provided it is remembered that this is simply a distinction of convenience or terminology—rather than of real substance—there can seemingly be no objection.

This chapter deals with certain offences involving motor vehicles which are prosecuted under the general criminal law rather than those aspects of it designed to regulate traffic, vehicles or standards of driving. Such offences may also involve endorsement of a licence and/or disqualification from driving. Generally, where not straightforward: 📖✋

THEFT OF MOTOR VEHICLES

There is no specific or separate offence of *stealing* a motor vehicle. Theft of property in general is a statutory offence under section 1 Theft Act 1968. It is purely incidental if a vehicle is involved.

Theft of, say, a car should be distinguished from the lesser offence of taking a motor vehicle without the owner's consent, below. Theft involves *inter alia* acting dishonestly and an intention to permanently deprive the owner of his or her property, which taking without consent does not. Under its full definition, theft is committed where a person dishonestly appropriates property belonging to another with the intention of permanently depriving that other person of the property (in the present context his or her vehicle).

Dishonesty is determined by applying a subjective test, i.e. looking at whether the accused's actions were dishonest according to the ordinary standards of reasonable and honest people, and then asking whether the accused realised that his or her actions were, according to those standards, dishonest. The requirement of an intention to permanently deprive the owner excludes situations where a person 'borrows' a motor vehicle, even when this is without permission. 'Borrowing' without permission may amount to taking without consent—or even aggravated vehicle-taking (see below).

Theft is an either-way offence, with a maximum penalty on summary conviction of six months imprisonment and/or a Level 5 fine (i.e. maximum £5,000). The Crown Court maxima are seven years imprisonment and/or an unlimited fine.

Disqualification for stealing or attempting to steal a motor vehicle
On conviction for stealing or attempting to steal a motor vehicle, the court may disqualify the offender from driving for any period, but there is *no endorsement* and *no penalty points* are recorded—by way of exception to the general rule that discretionary disqualification and the fact that an offence is endorsable go hand in hand (see, generally, *Chapter 8*).

GOING EQUIPPED TO STEAL

As in relation to theft, there is no separate offence of going equipped to steal a motor vehicle. Section 25 Theft Act 1968, provides that someone is guilty of an offence if, when not at his place of abode, he has with him any article (such as a bunch of ignition keys) for use in the course of, or in connection with, any burglary, theft or cheat. For the purposes of section 25, theft includes taking a conveyance without the owner's consent (even though, as already explained, this does not amount to theft under section 1 of the 1968 Act: see further below).

The court must be satisfied that the alleged offender had the article for use in some future theft such as the theft of a motor vehicle or its contents. It is not necessary for the prosecution to prove that the defendant intended to use the article personally. Once possession of it has been proved, there is an evidential burden on the accused to show that the article was in his or her possession for purposes other than a theft, burglary or cheat.

Going equipped is an either-way offence with a maximum penalty on summary conviction of six months imprisonment and/or a Level 5 fine (i.e. £5,000). The Crown Court maxima are three years imprisonment and/or an unlimited fine.

Disqualification
On conviction for going equipped to steal or to take a motor vehicle without consent, the court may disqualify for any period, but, as with theft of a vehicle, there is no endorsement and no penalty points are recorded.

VEHICLE INTERFERENCE

Under section 9 Criminal Attempts Act 1981, there is a specific summary offence of interferring with vehicles. The offence is committed if someone interferes with a motor vehicle or trailer or with anything carried in or on a motor vehicle or trailer with the intention that a specified offence shall be committed by him or some other person. The specified offences are:

- theft of the motor vehicle or trailer, or part of it; or
- theft of anything carried in or on the motor vehicle or trailer; or
- any offence of taking and driving the motor vehicle without consent.

The prosecutor does not have to prove exactly which offence the defendant intended—he or she must merely need to show that the defendant's intention was to either take the vehicle, or steal it or steal from inside it.

The offence is a purely summary one and the maximum penalty is imprisonment for a term not exceeding three months and/or to a fine not exceeding Level 4 (i.e. £2,500). It does *not* carry endorsement or disqualification.

TAKING WITHOUT CONSENT

Under section 12(1) Theft Act 1968, it is an offence

- to take unauthorised possession or control of a conveyance without the owner's consent or other lawful authority, for one's own use (or for another's use); or
- knowing that any such conveyance has been taken without such authority, to drive it or allow oneself to be carried in or on it.

This is a summary only offence (often called 'TWC' or 'TWOC': hence 'twocking'). The maximum penalty is six months imprisonment and/or a fine not exceeding Level 5 (i.e. £5,000).

It should be noted that the provisions refer not to vehicles but 'conveyances'. Conveyances include motor vehicles and mechanically propelled vehicles, and also any conveyance constructed or adapted for the carriage of people by land, water or air, i.e. including boats and aircraft. Note also that it is an offence to drive a conveyance, or allow oneself to be carried in or on it, knowing that the conveyance has been taken without authority. The prosecutor must prove actual knowledge of the taking.

The offence is complete once the conveyance is taken. In other words, there must be some evidence of movement and that the vehicle was used as a conveyance. It could, e.g. be committed if an unauthorised person entered a vehicle and released the hand brake so that it rolled down a hill. Here, the conveyance is used as a form of transport, albeit not *driven* in the conventional sense. However, if somebody pushed a neighbour's car out to clear access to their driveway, the offence may not have been committed. More typically, the offence is committed where someone takes a car for their own use, or for use in connection with some other crime (say to avoid identification), or for the purposes of what has become known as joy-riding. The surrounding circumstances can be quite serious or dangerous. However, such other matter should be charged separately and with this offence, taking without consent, the court is concerned only with matters which directly affect the seriousness of the taking. Nonetheless, seriousness can still vary widely. As always, the precise facts must always be examined in a given case.

Statutory defence
There is a statutory defence to taking without consent if the court is satisfied that the accused acted in the belief that he or she had lawful authority, or that the owner would have consented had he or she known of the circumstances of the taking. It is up to the accused to raise the defence (usually by giving or calling evidence) and then the onus remains on the prosecutor to establish, beyond reasonable doubt, the lack of such belief or consent.

Disqualification
On conviction for taking a motor vehicle without consent (including driving it, or allowing oneself to be carried on it) the court may disqualify, but there is no endorsement and no penalty points are recorded.

Possible interplay with other offending
Courts should be aware that there may sometimes be a 'trade off' between defendants to avoid responsibility/liability. A car taken without consent avoids, e.g. any question of whether the driver was insured vis-à-vis the owner. Similarly, an allegation that a car has been taken without consent may enable an owner to escape personal liability for an offence such as driving whilst disqualified, or more serious crimes. Whilst such scenarios do not occur every day, they do from time to time—when magistrates are likely to be confronted with a situation which is less than straightforward, or which may stretch belief.

AGGRAVATED VEHICLE-TAKING

As a result of public concern, this offence was created by the Aggravated Vehicle-Taking Act 1992. That Act inserted a new section 12A into the Theft Act 1968. Aggravated vehicle-taking is an either-way offence, applicable only to mechanically propelled vehicles (and not to all conveyances: contrast taking without consent above). The offence is committed if:

(a) the basic offence of taking a motor vehicle without consent is committed; and

(b) at any time after the vehicle was so taken, and before it was recovered, it was driven, or injury or damage was caused in one or more of the following circumstances:
   (i) the vehicle was driven dangerously on a road or other public place (dangerous driving has the same meaning as in *Chapter* 2);
   (ii) owing to the driving of the vehicle, an accident occurred by which injury was caused to any person (it is not necessary for the prosecutor to show any fault on the part of the driver);
   (iii) owing to the driving of the vehicle an accident occurred whereby damage was caused to any property other than the vehicle (it is not necessary for the prosecutor to show any fault on the part of the driver);
   (iv) damage was caused to the vehicle.

Statutory defence to aggravated vehicle-taking

There is a statutory defence if the accused proves that the driving, accident or damage occurred before he or she committed the basic offence, or that he or she was not in the immediate vicinity of the vehicle when the dangerous driving, injury or damage took place.

Penalty for aggravated vehicle-taking

In the magistrates' court, this either-way offence is subject to a maximum sentence of six months imprisonment and/or a fine not exceeding Level 5 (i.e. £5,000). Where the only allegation apart from the unlawful taking of the mechanically propelled vehicle is damage to the property or the vehicle concerned and the total value does not exceed £5,000, the offence is triable *only* by the magistrates.

In the Crown Court, the maximum penalty is two years imprisonment and/or unlimited fine, except where the accident caused the death of a person when the maximum imprisonment is increased to five years.

Before both the magistrates' court and Crown Court, there must, on conviction, be a minimum of 12 months obligatory disqualification from driving (in the absence of special reasons: see, generally, *Chapter 8*).

Sentencing guidelines issued by the Magistrates' Association suggest that consideration of a custodial sentence will be the usual approach following a conviction. Factors which aggravate the seriousness of the offence include prolonged high speed chases with the police, alcohol consumption and ignoring a passenger's plea to stop.

Helpful guidelines on the approach to be adopted with regard to the sentencing of drivers and passengers convicted under Section 12A have been provided by the Court of Appeal when dealing with disparity both apparent and real. In *R v. Harper* [1995] RTR 340 it was stated that all other things being equal, a passenger in a case of aggravated vehicle-taking could expect to receive a lesser sentence than the driver. Similarly, in *R v.*

Gosthowski [1995] RTR 324 it was held that the disqualification imposed on the passenger ought to have been in the order of half the disqualification imposed upon the driver.

DISHONESTY AND DOCUMENT OFFENCES

Chapter 4 discusses a number of special offences, including the fraudulent use of an excise licence under section 44 Vehicle Excise and Registration Act 1994, forging an appropriate licence or document under section 44 of the 1994 Act and the forgery etc. of documents under the Road Traffic Act 1988. Such activities can also be prosecuted under the general laws appertaining to dishonesty and forgery if appropriate or, say, under the law of conspiracy if large scale activity is involved.

CHAPTER 6

Miscellaneous Offences

DRIVING WHILST DISQUALIFIED

Driving whilst disqualified is committed by anyone who, whilst disqualified from holding or obtaining a licence, either obtains a licence or drives a motor vehicle on a road: section 103 Road Traffic Act 1988. The offence is one of strict liability, i.e. it is not open to the defendant to say that he or she did not know of the disqualification. In *R v. Bowsher* [1973] RTR 202 the defendant was rightly convicted where his licence was returned to him early and in error. In *R v. Miller* [1975] RTR 479 no defence was available to a defendant who thought that the place where he was driving was not a road.

Proof of disqualification

Proof of the disqualification is essential to a conviction, but this has given rise to a good deal of case law beginning with *R v. Derwentside Justices, ex parte Heaviside* [1996] RTR 384 where the defendant's conviction was quashed by the High Court on the basis that the only evidence available of the disqualification was the production of the court register. The High Court ruled that strict proof of identity was required, and involves either an admission or finger print evidence, or evidence of someone present at the time of the disqualification who was able to identify the defendant. That case was followed by *R v. Derwentside Magistrates' Court, ex parte Swift* [1997] RTR 89, where the High Court said that the three methods of proving identity mentioned above were not an exhaustive list and, therefore, to some extent the issue is causing less concern than before. Whilst strict proof of identity of the driver as the person who was previously disqualified *is* still required, the issue is really one of the sufficiency of the evidence. Interestingly, in the later case of *Director of Public Prosecutions v. Mansfield* [1997] RTR 96, Mr Justice Rougier said that there would invariably be sufficient evidence to at least establish a *prima facie* case, and once this was done, then either the defendant gave evidence and could be questioned, or alternatively he exercised his right to stay silent in the trial and adverse conclusions could be drawn if necessary: 🕮✋

The offence is only committed if the vehicle is *driven* on a road. Simply being *in charge* of a vehicle is not sufficient. It is also possible for the offence to be aided and abetted where knowledge of the disqualification exists on the part of the person allowing the principal offender to drive.

If someone is disqualified until he or she passes a driving test (*Chapter 8*), he or she may immediately apply for a provisional licence and is entitled to drive once the application has been received (subject to complying with the conditions of such a licence, e.g. displaying L-plates and being accompanied by a qualified driver).

It is an offence for someone disqualified from holding or obtaining a driving licence *to obtain* a licence whilst so disqualified. This will not prevent the person who is disqualified from applying shortly prior to the end of a disqualification for the return of his or her driving licence on the due date, but, since licences are sometimes sent out before the commencement date, it is essential for the recipient to check carefully on when his or her entitlement to drive re-starts.

Arrest

Driving whilst disqualified is an arrestable offence, i.e. a constable may arrest at any time any person driving a motor vehicle on a road whom he or she has reasonable cause to suspect of being disqualified. Driving whilst disqualified and obtaining a driving licence whilst disqualified are summary only offences. One consequence of this is that the Criminal Attempts Act 1981 (which applies to indictable offences, including either way offences) no longer applies to these offences. Attempting to drive whilst disqualified and attempting to obtain a licence whilst disqualified are, therefore, no longer themselves criminal offences.

Proceedings and penalties

The offence can be prosecuted within three years of being committed, but proceedings must be started within six months from the date when, in the prosecutor's opinion, he or she has sufficient evidence to warrant proceedings. Driving whilst disqualified is a purely summary offence punishable by a Level 5 fine (i.e. maximum £5,000) and/or six months imprisonment. The offence is endorsable. It carries six penalty points and discretionary disqualification.

SPEEDING

The Road Traffic Regulation Act 1984 divides offences of exceeding the speed limit into four categories:

- exceeding the limit on a road restricted to 30, 40 or 50 miles per hour

- exceeding the temporary limits of 50, 60 and 70 miles per hour on roads other than motorways
- exceeding the limits applicable to the class of a vehicle on any road
- exceeding the speed limits applicable to motorways.

Corroboration

By virtue of section 89(2) of the 1984 Act a defendant cannot be convicted solely on the evidence of one witness stating that the defendant was driving at a speed exceeding the limit, i.e. his or her opinion. It is one of the few offences in law where corroboration is legally essential before there can be a conviction. Corroboration is, therefore, always required, except in relation to an allegation of exceeding the overall speed limit on a motorway. This is specifically provided by section 17 of the 1984 Act.

The most familiar forms of corroboration include the speedometer in a police car, radar, VASCAR and video camera. Less common forms of corroboration include evidence from skid marks or damage sustained by a vehicle.

In practice, prosecutions for speeding based on the evidence of two police officers, or the opinion of a police officer corroborated by a speedometer are a rarity nowadays—but are still encountered. The use of radar is also significantly diminished, and the most likely method of detection/evidence is some form of hand held electronic device or evidence from an automatic camera located by the roadside.

Technology

Hand held radar guns are used by most police forces. Operated by a single police officer, such devices provide the corroboration required by law. The names of the devices most commonly used are Muniquip and GATSO. The gun is pointed at the moving vehicle, the radar beam strikes the vehicle and the gun measures the change when the beam is reflected back to it. The speed of the vehicle is displayed and can be shown to the driver. Such guns have a range of 500 metres or more.

Readings have been challenged in the courts and it is essential that the guidance manual is followed to the letter. Evidence of this will need to be given if the reading or use of the device is disputed.

Laser technology has now been introduced into hand held devices, and the resulting narrow beam allows greater accuracy in targeting individual vehicles. Such equipment will operate up to distances of one kilometre, and will be commonly used over distances well in excess of 500 metres. Statistically, this provides a very accurate method of measuring speed. Computer technology is contained within a VASCAR (visual average speed computer and recorder). This can be operated from stationary or moving vehicles and is dependent upon the constable's accuracy in operating switches, when a vehicle being measured passes particular points on the road.

Obstructing the police

The flashing of headlights is often witnessed on roads as an indication that speed checks are being carried out. Such conduct can amount to obstructing the police in the execution of their duty, and form the basis of a prosecution: see *Green v. Moore* [1982] 1 All ER 428.

Speed limits

Whether a road is a 'restricted road' and a particular limit is in operation, and whether a motorist could have known the limit in question is the subject of legislation and much case law. Where such points arise, magistrates will need to consider guidance before proceeding: 📖✋

Temporary minimum and maximum speed limits are permitted by the regulations. The most common is the temporary maximum speed limit for road works.

Speed limits are also applicable to different classes of vehicle, including:

- passenger vehicles and motor caravans
- goods vehicles
- dual purpose vehicles
- articulated vehicles and tractors
- agricultural vehicles.

These are all prescribed, and the relevant definitions need close examination in a given case. Advice is essential if a contentious point is raised: 📖✋

Proceedings and penalty

The Road Traffic Offenders Act 1988 requires a warning of prosecution for speeding offences to be given to an alleged offender. Offences of speeding are commonly met by the issue of a fixed penalty notice. When prosecuted in this way, the offence is endorsable and carries a fixed three penalty points. For fixed penalties generally, see *Chapter 9*.

When prosecuted in court, the offence is a summary only offence with subject to a Level 3 fine (i.e. maximum £1,000) with the exception of exceeding the overall speed limit for a motorway, which carries a Level 4 fine (maximum £2,500). The offence is endorsable with variable penalty points on the range 3 to 6. Disqualification is discretionary.

Failure to comply with a *minimum* speed limit is not endorsable.

TRAFFIC LIGHTS

Duty to stop at red light

According to the regulations, when the red light shows this 'signal shall convey the prohibition that vehicular traffic other than tram cars shall not proceed beyond the stop line'. What happens if the front of the vehicle has already crossed the stop line when the light changes to red? The driver may not proceed further without committing an offence.

Red and amber

The prohibition referred to above in relation to a red signal is not altered when the red and amber signal is showing.

Amber

It is no offence under the regulations to disobey the amber signal alone, which strictly speaking conveys the same prohibition as the red signal except that if the vehicle is so close to the stop line that it cannot safely be stopped the driver may proceed.

The stop line

The significance of the stop line is of interest. If there is no stop line or it is not visible, the driver must use the sign indicating 'when red light shows wait here' if any, and if there is no such sign then the traffic light post itself must be used. Occasionally, instances are met where the lights are for some reason not working. It is doubtful whether it is lawful to proceed where lights are apparently stuck at red. In such circumstances it is not unusual for drivers to proceed with caution, but freedom from prosecution in such circumstances, e.g. if an accident occurs, cannot be guaranteed. Such a prosecution could, e.g. be for careless driving (see *Chapter* 2).

Operation of signals

Occasionally, a situation will arise where part of a set of traffic lights is not working. Regulations indicate that 'any reference to light signals, to the signals or to a signal of a particular colour, is, where secondary signals have been placed, a reference to the light signals displayed by both the primary and secondary signals or, as the case may be, by the primary signals operating without the secondary signals, or by the secondary signals operating without the primary signals'. Where both primary and secondary lights are established, the regulation seems to suggest that it will be sufficient for the purpose of prosecution that one of the sets is working, and not necessarily both. This point and others that might conceivably arise as a result of this regulation have not yet resulted in decided cases.

Wells v. Woodward (1956) 54 LGR 142 and *Pacitty v. Copeland* (1963) SLT (Notes) 52 are authority for saying that courts may take it for granted that if lights are showing green for east-west traffic, then they are red for north-south traffic unless the contrary is proved.

Technology

The Highways Act 1980 empowers local authorities to locate cameras near traffic lights in order to detect offences. These are now familiar sights across the country, and offences will usually result in a fixed penalty notice being issued: see, generally, *Chapter 9*. The effect of the installation of cameras (the same applies in respect of speed cameras) is of interest. Once it is known that a particular camera is operational in an area, attitudes towards offending within sight of the camera change noticeably. It is clear, however, that the enormity of the task of analysing the contents of the films, and processing the results is such that cameras are far more likely to be without film than to be operational. The mere fact of their presence at the roadside, however, is sufficient to deter motorists from taking a chance on whether or not the camera is loaded with film.

Penalty

The basic offence of failing to comply with automatic traffic lights is punishable on summary conviction only. It carries a Level 3 fine (i.e. maximum £1,000), is endorsable with 3 penalty points and carries discretionary disqualification.

PEDESTRIAN AND SCHOOL CROSSINGS

The Zebra Pedestrian Crossing Regulations 1971 govern uncontrolled or zebra crossings. Zebra crossings are familiar for their black and white stripes, the boundaries of which are indicated by lines of studs across the carriageway. The other familiar feature of such crossings is the yellow light mounted on black and white posts. These are required to be sited on either side of the road and illuminated by flashing lights. Where the crossing is divided by a central refuge, there is no requirement for a yellow light to be placed on the refuge, although this may occur. The other common feature of such crossings is the familiar zig-zag markings stretching back for a distance on either side of the crossing.

Controlled or pelican pedestrian crossings are governed by the 1987 Regulations. These are again familiar landmarks, and are identified by traffic lights with the zig-zag markings referred to above. The principal offences in relation to pedestrian crossings are:

- failing to accord precedence to pedestrians
- stopping in a zebra controlled area
- overtaking in a zebra controlled area.

Failing to accord precedence

The offence of failing to accord precedence to pedestrians at zebra crossings is committed only if pedestrians are on the carriageway, within the limits of the crossing, before the vehicle or any part of it has come on the carriageway within those limits, i.e. the black and white striped crossing itself. There is, therefore, no requirement in law to stop to allow a pedestrian waiting on the kerb to cross. Once, however, the pedestrian steps onto the crossing itself, the car is obliged to stop. Where a central reservation is in existence, the crossing is to be treated as if in two separate halves. There is a significant body of case law which deals with failure to accord precedence, and in appropriate circumstances advice will be needed: 📖✋

A driver is required to approach a crossing in such a manner that he or she is able to stop in the event that a pedestrian steps onto it. Rulings of the High Court have strictly applied the regulation by placing an absolute duty upon the driver. The circumstances or explanation can, of course, be reflected in the penalty or lack of it.

Another commonly met situation is that presented by another road user on wheels using the pedestrian crossing. An example would be someone with a push-bike. The question for the court to decide will be whether the pedestrian is using the crossing as a foot passenger. If, e.g. the cyclist pushes the cycle across the crossing, he or she is acting as a pedestrian. If, however, they are riding or even using the cycle as a scooter, they will not be acting as a pedestrian.

Restrictions on stopping

Stopping in a zebra controlled area—identified by the zig-zag lines on the road on either side of the crossing—is also an offence, provided the circumstances are not beyond the driver's control. Fire engines, ambulances and police are amongst those exempted from the provisions prohibiting stopping in the controlled area.

Restriction on overtaking

It is also an offence to overtake another moving motor vehicle or a stationary vehicle in the zebra controlled area, *on the approach* to such a crossing. For the avoidance of doubt, it is not an offence to overtake in the controlled area *on the far side* of the crossing. Once the vehicle being overtaken is beyond the limits of the crossing (i.e. the studs) and, therefore, in reality onto the black and white striped part of the crossing, no offence is committed by the overtaking vehicle, since the vehicle overtaken was on the crossing itself and not in the controlled area.

An offence will only be committed by overtaking a stationary vehicle if that vehicle stopped for the purpose of complying with the regulations, the principal reason for which will be to allow pedestrians to cross, whether the pedestrian is actually on the crossing or waiting to cross.

Note that in all these cases the offence is only committed by overtaking a moving motor vehicle not, e.g. a bicycle.

In the case of pelican pedestrian crossings, stopping within the controlled area is prohibited (i.e. the zig-zags), as is stopping within the limits of the crossing itself.

All these offences are summary only, and the majority are punishable by a Level 3 fine (i.e. maximum £1,000). They are endorsable with three penalty points and attract discretionary disqualification.

School crossings

School crossings are dealt with under the Road Traffic Regulation Act 1984. When required to do so by the school crossing patrol sign, the driver must stop his or her vehicle before reaching the place where the children are crossing or seeking to cross, so as not to stop or impede their crossing. The vehicle must not be put in motion again whilst the sign continues to be exhibited. Offences can only be committed between 8.00 a.m. and 5.30 p.m.

In *Franklyn v. Langdown* [1971] RTR 471 a party consisting of children and adults were crossing the road under the protection of the school crossing patrol sign. With the children over the crown of the road, the defendant drove out of a side road, passing behind the last of the adults and causing her to move more quickly. The school crossing patrol sign was still in place. The magistrates dismissed the case, but the High Court directed a conviction, since the words 'and so as not to stop or impede their crossing' merely describe the manner in which the motorist is required to stop.

Other points considered in case law dealing with these regulations have included the manner in which the sign is displayed by the crossing patrol warden, the nature and colour of the sign and the wearing of the approved uniform. Issues could also arise on the definition of 'school', 'road' and 'children', as well as whether traffic wardens may undertake school crossing patrol duties. Again, where such issues are raised, reference to case law, the regulations or the statute is required: 📖✋

Penalty

The principal offence of failing to stop at a school crossing is purely summary, and punishable by a Level 3 fine (i.e. maximum £1,000). It is endorsable with three penalty points and attracts discretionary disqualification.

VEHICLE IN DANGEROUS POSITION

The offence of leaving a vehicle in a dangerous position is committed by someone causing or permitting a vehicle or trailer to remain at rest on a road so as to involve a danger of injury to other persons using the road. Before proceeding, a notice of intended prosecution is required: see *Appendix C*. With the growth in the number of vehicles using our roads, this is certainly an offence of which greater use could be made. In an effort to find a place to park, set against a background of significant parking restrictions, it is common to see vehicles parked dangerously. A typical example is parking a vehicle on a blind corner. In *Maguire v. Crouch* (1941) 104 JP 445 a conviction was upheld in respect of a vehicle left in a safe position but without the hand brake set, causing it to move off.

Leaving a vehicle in a dangerous position is a summary offence with a maximum fine on Level 3 (i.e. maximum £1,000). It is endorsable with three penalty points and attracts discretionary disqualification.

OBSTRUCTING THE HIGHWAY

Obstructing the highway can be prosecuted under a number of different statutory provisions. Whether the placing of a vehicle on a highway amounts to an obstruction is a question of fact and degree in all the circumstances. A large body of case law has grown up around the vexed question of obstruction. Examples of where defendants have been properly convicted of obstruction in one form or another, have included the following:

- making a forbidden U-turn and holding up traffic in a busy street for 50 seconds
- parking bumper to bumper with the car in front, so that when another car parked on the other side, leaving a gap of two feet, the car in the middle could not move
- parking a van for five minutes in a wide busy street near to a bus stop, and refusing to move.

The following have been held not to amount to unnecessary obstruction on their given facts:

- parking a vehicle in a bus bay for five minutes without any evidence of a bus trying to park at that time (a bill-poster parked his van with two wheels on the footpath and the other two on the road, whilst carrying out his activities);
- parking unattended for five minutes, so as to block out one of four lines of traffic in a street carrying a tram route.

From the decided cases it can be seen that the test frequently applied is one of reasonableness, again one of fact and degree depending upon all the circumstances. In *Nagy v. Weston* [1965] 1 All ER 78, Lord Parker said:

> . . . while there must be proof of unreasonable use, whether or not user amounting to obstruction was or was not unreasonable use was a question of fact, depending upon all the circumstances, including the length of time the obstruction continued, the place where it occurred, the purpose for which it was done, and whether it caused an actual as opposed to potential obstruction.

It is noteworthy that a number of the cases on this subject arise out of the magistrates' decision to acquit (sometimes on a submission of no case to answer), and a subsequent appeal to the High Court which resulted in the case being sent back to magistrates with a direction either to proceed or to convict. This significant amount of case law is indicative of the fact that guidance will often be needed, and for even stronger reasons where issues of law are raised: 🕮 ✋

Penalties

Obstruction of the highway under the Highways Act 1980 is punishable with a fine on Level 3 (i.e. £1,000). Obstruction of a road is punishable under the Road Traffic Act 1988 with a Level 4 fine (£2,500). Both offences are summary only and neither carries endorsement.

MOTORWAY OFFENCES

The use of motorways is restricted to those in Classes I and II in Schedule 4 to the Highways Act 1980. Motorists will be familiar with signs indicating the start of motorways. Learner drivers and motor cyclists with engines less than 50cc are examples of excluded categories. An offence is committed by using a motorway in breach of the regulations/prohibitions. The following are examples:

Stopping on the motorway

Some of the most frequent offences relating to motor vehicles on the motorway involve the restrictions on stopping. A vehicle may legitimately stop on the hard shoulder for reasons of emergency or other circumstances set out in the regulations. It is, however, an offence for a vehicle to be driven or to stop on a hard shoulder unless these circumstances apply. Accidents or other emergencies are the most common exemptions from prosecution. In *Higgins v. Bernard* [1972] RTR 304 a motorist began to feel drowsy when he was a mile from the start of the motorway. He could find nowhere to park his car. Knowing that he was ten miles away from the next motorway exit, he parked on the slip road. It was directed that he should be convicted, as he felt drowsy before he had reached the motorway slip road.

Reversing and using the central reservation and learner drivers

Other offences commonly met are reversing, using the central reservation or verge and breach of the prohibition of use by learner drivers.

Penalties

The principal motorway offences are all punishable only on summary conviction and by a Level 4 fine (maximum £2,500). They are endorsable with three penalty points and attract discretionary disqualification. By way of exception, unlawfully stopping or parking on the hard shoulder is *not* endorsable, in contrast to the offence of stopping on the carriageway which *is* endorsable.

CONSTRUCTION AND USE REGULATIONS

The Construction and Use Regulations deal with the maintenance of brakes, steering gear and tyres, the condition of the vehicle and loads, amongst other things. Contravention of these regulations is an offence under section 41A Road Traffic Offenders Act 1988. The regulations need careful and detailed consideration, since they have been widely amended and also need to be considered in the light of EC provisions. Always seek advice in less than straightforward situations: 🕮 ✋

Brakes

Put simply, the requirement is that brakes must be capable of stopping a vehicle within a reasonable distance under the most adverse conditions. The *Highway Code* (see *Chapter 1*) sets out braking distances. The commentary on the braking distances provides as follows:

> The safe rule is never to get closer than the overall stopping distances shown. In good conditions on roads carrying fast traffic, a two second time gap may be sufficient. The gap should be at least doubled on wet roads and increased further on icy roads. Large vehicles and motor cycles need more time to stop than cars. Drop back if someone overtakes, and pulls into the gap in front of you.

There is extensive case law on the subject of brakes, and what follows is a brief summary. In *Kennett v. British Airports Authority* [1975] RTR 164, the magistrates dismissed a defective brakes allegation because, overall, the system was efficient. The High Court, however, directed a conviction because the disc brake on one wheel was badly worn. The regulations provide that *every part* of the system must be maintained in good and efficient working order and properly adjusted. *Bailey v. Rolfe* (1976) Crim. LR 77 confirms that the standard of proof is proof beyond reasonable doubt, i.e. the prosecutor must prove to this generally applicable standard that the vehicle's brakes were not maintained as the regulations require.

The user is obliged to ensure that the brakes have been maintained in a good and efficient working order, and this obligation is an absolute one: *Green v. Burnett* [1954] 3 All ER 273. In *Hawkins v. Holmes* [1974] RTR 436 it was held not to be a defence for the defendant to say that he had ensured the brakes were regularly maintained, or that he had done all that he could do to see that the brakes were in order: but see later for the ability of the defendant to avoid endorsement in certain circumstances, through lack of knowledge.

Stoneley v. Richardson [1973] RTR 229 is authority for the proposition that a constable, as opposed to an authorised examiner, is entitled to give evidence as to the efficiency of the braking system. In that case, the officer was able to push the defendant's car along the road, even with the hand brake fully applied. The High Court directed the magistrates to convict. In the majority of cases, the question of whether or not brakes are maintained in good and efficient working order will be a simple question of fact. Technical evidence, though sometimes called, is not generally needed.

On conviction, the offence carries a Level 5 fine (maximum £5,000) in respect of goods vehicles or vehicles adapted to carry more than 8 passengers, and a Level 4 fine (£2,500) in every other case. The offence is punishable on summary conviction only. It carries obligatory endorsement of three penalty points and discretionary disqualification.

Vehicle or load in dangerous condition

Under section 40A Road Traffic Offenders Act 1988 it is an offence for someone to use, cause or permit another to use a motor vehicle or trailer on a road when either:

(a) the condition of the motor vehicle or trailer or of its accessories or equipment; or
(b) the purpose for which it is used; or
(c) the number of passengers carried by it or the manner in which they are carried; or
(d) the weight, position or distribution of its load or the manner in which it is secured is such that the use of the motor vehicle or trailer involves a danger of injury to any person.

The offence is punishable on summary conviction by a fine on Level 5 (maximum £5,000) if the vehicle is a goods vehicle, or one adapted to carry more than 8 passengers, and a Level 4 fine (maximum £2,500) in any other case. The offence carries obligatory endorsement with three penalty points and attracts discretionary disqualification.

Insecure and dangerous loads

An important distinction between an insecure load and a dangerous load is that the former is not endorsable if no danger is proved. Regulation 100 of the Construction and Use Regulations creates the various offences and the wording of the provisions bears careful consideration. Again, case law is plentiful:

In *Cornish v. Ferrymasters Ltd.* [1975] RTR 292 a drum fell off a lorry onto the road because the palette upon which it was loaded collapsed for some unexplicable reason. Both the owners and the driver were charged with using, and the magistrates dismissed both allegations. The High Court, however, directed that both be convicted since the offence of using is an absolute one, and knowledge or lack of it is irrelevant. Knowledge was also irrelevant to the likelihood or otherwise of danger being caused. In contrast, however, where an *employer* is charged with permitting a vehicle to be used with an insecure load, the prosecutor is required to prove that a director, i.e. someone with appropriate knowledge, knew of the breach of the regulation. In *Gifford v. Whittaker* [1942] 1 All ER 604 a driver was rightly convicted where crates fell off a lorry, even though they had been loaded by someone else.

An overhanging load may also result in conviction pursuant to Regulation 100. Examples have included trees overhanging the back of a trailer and part of a bulldozer protruding three feet beyond the offside of the carrying vehicle: *Newstead v. Hern* (1950) 114 JPN 690. In *Reeve v. Webb* [1973] RTR 130, a motorcyclist had extended his exhaust so as to cause potential danger to anyone touching it whilst hot, or suffering the consequences of exhaust fumes. This was held to be an offence under the regulation.

Regulation 100 is widely drawn and potentially overlaps with other regulations. So, e.g. in *Bason v. Eayrs* (1958) Crim. LR 397 excessive play of up to one-third in the steering could properly be dealt with under regulation 100, as opposed to being prosecuted as 'defective steering'.

The regulation refers to parts and accessories of vehicles and trailers. Two cases, *Jenkins v. Dean* (1933) 78 SJ 13 and *Keyse v. Sainsbury* [1971] 2 RTR 218, held that chains and a weighted attachment at the rear of a tractor were not part of the vehicle, and accordingly convictions should not follow as charged.

Regulation 100(2) requires a load to be properly secured. A prosecution under sub-regulation (1) was wrong in the case of *MacDermott Movements Ltd. v. Horsfield* [1983] RTR 42 where a high load had slipped. It was decided that the load would not have been too high had it been properly secured, and hence the slippage was the offending feature.

Finally, regulation 100(3) prevents the use of a motor vehicle for a purpose for which it is unsuitable so as to cause, or to be likely to cause, danger. If a lorry's load is so badly stacked as to cause the lorry to topple over, it does not follow that the vehicle itself is unsuitable to carry that load: see *Hollis Brothers v. Bailey* (1968) 112 SJ 381.

Tyres

Using a vehicle with defective tyres is an offence under section 41A Road Traffic Act 1988. A vehicle is in use if generally speaking it is parked on a road. The use, however, is the use that the vehicle is being put to at the particular time, and so it is not necessary for tyres to be kept inflated for some future use: see *Conner v. Graham* [1981] RTR 291.

R v. Tiverton Justices [1980] RTR 280 is an important case: authority for a general principle in relation to magistrates' courts, albeit that it happened to be a case involving defective tyres. The magistrates retired and took with them a tyre gauge to carry out a private test on a tyre. They were held to be wrong in that they were in breach of their duty to hear the whole case in open court.

Regulation 27 Construction and Use Regulations provides eight different types of defect. Each tyre must be the subject of a separate information in respect of any of these defects.

All motorists will be familiar with bald tyres caused by defective tracking. A tyre which can appear to be legal may be caught by regulation 27 in a number of ways, particularly where the grooves of the tread pattern of the tyre have not got a depth of at least one millimetre throughout a continuous band measuring at least three quarters of the breadth of the tread and around the entire circumference of the tyre. Reference to the entire outer circumference means that part of the tyre normally in contact with the road—and does not include the outer walls and the shoulder of the tyre. It is *not* essential that the tyre is examined by an authorised examiner: *Phillips v. Thomas* [1974] RTR 28. In this case, it was held that the question of whether a tyre complies with the regulations is one of fact, and it is not essential for the police constable who examined the tyre and gave evidence to be an authorised examiner.

Another case dealing with a commonly met procedural point is *R v. Sandwell Justices* (1979) Crim. LR 56. In that case, the allegations referred to the tyre in question as the one on the *rear nearside.* At court, the police officer gave evidence that the tyre in question was on the *rear offside.* The magistrates allowed an amendment to the information, notwithstanding that what is now section 127 Magistrates' Courts Act 1980 would have prohibited a fresh information at the time. The High Court was asked to issue an order prohibiting the magistrates from further hearing the allegations, but this application was dismissed. The rationale was that the particular tyre was the only one involved, and the defendants knew which one it was. No injustice could, therefore, have been caused by the original description in the information.

Each offence relating to a defective tyre is punishable, on summary conviction, with a Level 4 fine (£2,500) in respect of all vehicles except goods vehicles and those adapted to carry more than 8 passengers, when it attracts a Level 5 fine (£5,000). The offence attracts obligatory endorsement of three penalty points and discretionary disqualification.

Non-endorsement

Knowledge in each of these cases under the Construction and Use Regulations is important in relation to the question of endorsement and, therefore, penalty points and possible disqualification. Endorsement must be ordered unless there are special reasons (see *Chapter 7*), or unless the defendant did not know and had no reason to suspect that an offence was being committed of using a motor vehicle or trailer or causing or permitting such use:

(a) so as to cause or be likely to cause danger for the condition of the vehicle or its parts or accessories, the number of passengers carried by it, or the weight distribution, packing or adjustment of its load;
(b) in breach of a requirement as to brakes, steering gear or tyres;
(c) for any purpose for which it is so unsuitable as to cause or be likely to cause danger.

Note that the court must not order the defendant to be disqualified, or penalty points to be endorsed on the driving licence if proof of the above is given. The defendant's evidence will be required on oath or affirmation, and he or she must show not only that they did not know of the defect, but also that they had no reasonable cause to suspect it. The question will be whether or not this particular defendant had reasonable cause. The onus will be upon the defendant to satisfy the court upon the balance of probabilities.

VEHICLE DEFECT RECTIFICATION SCHEMES

Vehicle defect rectification schemes (VDRS) can serve as an alternative to prosecution for people who are committing construction and use or vehicle lighting offences. There are many such schemes in operation across the country. Since their existence and means of operation do not depend on statute a great deal of variation exists in practice and readers should enquire locally: 📖✋

A typical objective of such a scheme is to ensure that once a defect has been identified by the police in, say, a roadside check, it is promptly repaired, thereby making the vehicle safe to be driven and reducing the risk of that particular vehicle being involved in an accident. Of equal value is the fact that the driver is given the opportunity of avoiding prosecution if the defect is satisfactorily repaired, thus releasing police officers from the time consuming duties of submitting process reports and having to attend court in comparatively minor cases.

Schemes will commonly apply to all motor vehicles, motor cycles and light commercial vehicles up to 1525 kgs unladen weight. They are unlikely to apply to hackney carriages, private hire vehicles, vehicles whose defects are caused as a result of an accident and which have contributed to an accident. They will also not apply when the driver is in unlawful possession of the vehicle.

When a vehicle is being checked and defects are discovered, the reporting officer will consider the seriousness of the defect and is likely to have discretion to give the motorist verbal advice or report for process. If the officer chooses the latter option, he or she will report the offender in the traditional manner. The driver will then be asked if he or she wishes to take advantage of the VDRS. The 'offender' will be able to avoid prosecution if the defects are rectified forthwith, and the vehicle is presented to an approved garage for inspection. Drivers may also decide to scrap the vehicle and, if so, written evidence of disposal should be forwarded, together with the VDRS paperwork to the appropriate police department.

The driver's responsibility is to ensure that the defects are rectified forthwith. If the examiner is satisfied that the defects have been rectified he or she will complete the paper work and return it to the driver. In order to avoid prosecution, the driver must ensure that the relevant paperwork is then returned to the police. The paperwork must similarly be completed if it is the registered keeper's decision to scrap the vehicle.

Where the vehicle owner is different from the driver, and the offences disclosed are those where the owner would be reported in addition to the driver (e.g. using, causing or permitting), then, if the driver does not comply with the conditions of the scheme, the owner will be given the opportunity to do so. Failure to do so may involve him or her in prosecution also.

Extension of the time limits is possible. For example, where a driver states that he or she cannot comply with the scheme because the vehicle has been stolen, the first duty of the police is to confirm this fact with the police national computer. Occasionally, the driver will state that the paperwork has been lost. In this event, copy paperwork can be sent to enable the scheme to be complied with. Sometimes the driver will indicate that the vehicle is being sold. The main purpose of the scheme is to ensure that the driver will rectify the vehicle, and in this instance no rectification has taken place, so the scheme has not been complied with.

Where the driver does not submit paperwork showing that the scheme *has* been complied with within the fourteen day period (or such extended period as allowed) this fact will be reported to the issuing officer who will finalise any further enquiries and submit a report for consideration for prosecution in the normal manner.

The operation of such schemes will result in a number of questions, and some typical points that arise are noted below:

- MOT test fees do not apply, but inspection and certification should be charged by the garage in accordance with normal business costing methods
- the garage is only responsible for the certification of the defects listed on the form, and not for any others that might arise during the course of the examination
- there is no requirement to have the vehicle rectified or repaired at an MOT garage. Arrangements for the repair of the vehicle can be made anywhere, even by the vehicle owner, as long as it is examined at an MOT testing station before final report
- the police will not examine the vehicle to save the offender going to an MOT garage
- the offender cannot keep the vehicle off the road until he or she can afford to repair it and in order to take advantage of the scheme and avoid prosecution, the vehicle must either be repaired or scrapped forthwith
- selling the vehicle will not avoid the obligation to comply
- the scheme will only be offered by the police to those motorists who are to be reported for vehicle defects and it does not take away an officer's discretion to advise or verbally warn a driver about minor vehicle defects.

DRIVERS' HOURS

Legislation governs drivers' hours in relation to the driving of certain vehicles such as motor coaches and goods vehicles. This legislation includes such matters as the maximum continuous driving period; maximum daily driving period and the daily rest period. There are duties imposed on both the employee and employer and these include keeping records. A variety of exemptions can apply and legal advice is necessary in considering the basic law, the keeping of records and tachograph offences: 🕮✋

Even where there is exemption from the need to use a tachograph (below), regulations may require manual records of journeys or work to be kept, for goods or passenger vehicles: 🕮✋

Tachographs: EC Rules

It is a legal requirement that a tachograph be installed and used in vehicles which are registered in a member state and used for the carriage of goods or passengers, by road. Traffic examiners and the police have power, at any time, to enter a vehicle and inspect any tachograph installed in it, and any tachograph record. There are exemptions from the regulations such as those in respect of public service vehicles for less than ten passengers, including the driver. Another example of an exemption is the one that applies to specialist vehicles used within Great Britain for a variety of different purposes (such as door-to-door selling).

A tachograph is a recording device which consists of a cable-fed combination of an odometer, a speedometer and a 24 hour clock. The time recorded on the tachograph must be in the time which agrees with the official time in the country of registration of the vehicle. Some of the activities it must be capable of recording include:

- speed
- distance travelled
- driving time
- other periods of work or of availability
- breaks from work and daily rest periods
- opening of the case containing the record sheet.

A tachograph may be installed in a vehicle or repaired only by fitters or workshops approved by a member state. The employer must issue crew members with enough tachograph sheets to cover their period of work. Completed sheets must be kept by the employer for a year. The employer may be required to produce them to an authorised inspector. The tachograph must be checked on installation, after each repair, and every two years.

Where there are two drivers, the tachograph must be capable of recording at the same time but distinctly and on two separate sheets, the driving time, other periods of work or availability, and breaks from work and daily rest periods.

The obligation on the driver is to ensure that the tachograph is kept running continuously and that times of driving, other periods of work and availability for work, breaks from work and rest periods are recorded.

The Divisional Court has ruled on a variety of appeals in respect of the EC Regulations concerning tachograph recording equipment. The cases include *Prime v. Hosking* (1994), *The Times*, December 30 where the defendant was a driver of a heavy goods vehicle. His contention in the High Court was that he should only be required to enter those periods when he was employed as a driver. This was not accepted. In this particular case, the defendant had ceased driving and then carried out 'overtime' labouring activity in his employer's yard. It was confirmed that the 'relevant working period' started when he took charge of his vehicle and ended when his day's work ended. The daily work period ceased when he completed his work. He was also not able to argue that the period of overtime constituted 'rest' within the regulations.

Another case, *Browne v. Anelay, The Times,* 10 June 1997 involved the High Court in ruling on the meaning of when a driver 'takes over a vehicle'. Here, the defendant had been one of two drivers employed to drive a coach from Scunthorpe to Warsaw. He boarded it at the start of the journey but was not due to drive until the coach reached Dover. It was held that he had started his working day and 'taken over the vehicle' (the wording in the regulations) by being present upon it when he boarded it at Scunthorpe. Accordingly, he should have started keeping tachograph records from then onwards. The regulations were intended to cover not only the person driving at the material time, but any other drivers present upon it who were drivers for the purpose of the journey the coach was making.

In *Director of Public Prosecutions v. Guy, The Times,* 3 July 1997 a driver was guilty of the offence of driving a vehicle when the tachograph was not working, even when he was driving home in his employer's vehicle—a tractor unit—having finished work for the day.

Employers are obliged to check their drivers' records. In *Wing v. Nuttall, The Times,* 30 April 1997 an employer who failed to make checks on the tachograph charts in order to confirm that drivers were complying with the relevant legal requirements was guilty of such reckless behaviour that knowledge of the contravention of the regulation was implied. A number of drivers had driven in excess of the hours allowed by the regulations and the coach owner was guilty of the offence of permitting these breaches. However, where a driver is guilty of falsification of tachograph records, the employer will only be convicted of aiding and abetting if he or she has knowledge of this.

Offences in relation to tachographs attract fines, but do not enable the court to endorse the defendant's licence, to disqualify or to award penalty points: 🕮✋

There are several statutory defences to allegations of contravening the tachograph regulations: 🕮✋ An example would be where someone is summoned for using a vehicle which was not fitted with a tachograph who was able to prove that at the time the vehicle was going to a place where an EC approved tachograph was to be installed.

The authors wish to acknowledge the assistance given to them by the Greater Manchester Police Force in compiling this chapter.

CHAPTER 7

Endorsement and Penalty Points

In addition to any penalty imposed by the court, certain motoring offences attract endorsement of the offender's driving licence or disqualification when the court *must*, by law, order that the defendant's driving licence is endorsed with:

- particulars of the offence, and
- the number of 'penalty points' appropriate to that offence.

The only exception is where a court finds *'Special reasons' for not endorsing:* see below. If no licence is held, the order operates as an order to endorse any licence which the offender obtains.

PENALTY POINTS

Every endorsable offence carries a number of penalty points, from a minimum of two to a maximum of eleven. Some of the more common offences and their points are:

Offence	Points
Careless or inconsiderate driving	3-9
In charge (offences relating to alcohol/drugs)	10
Failing to stop after an accident	5-10
Failing to report an accident	5-10
Driving whilst disqualified	6
Using etc. a motor vehicle whilst uninsured	6-8
Driving other than in accordance with a licence	3-6
Exceeding a speed limit	3-6
Failure to provide a preliminary specimen for a breath test	4
Failing to comply with traffic lights/directions	3
Construction and use offences	3
Contravention of pedestrian crossing regulations	3
Using a vehicle in a dangerous condition	3

Appendix B to this handbook contains a list of all endorsable offences and penalty points. The chief significance of the system lies in the 'totting up' provisions: see under *Obligatory Disqualification* in *Chapter 8*.

Variable points

Where the offences carries a range of points, the court has a discretion concerning the number to be endorsed—which will depend on the court's view of the seriousness of the offence.

Several offences

Where someone is convicted of two or more offences *committed* on the same occasion, the number of points to be endorsed is usually the highest number attracted by any one of the offences. Thus e.g. if an offender is convicted of driving while disqualified (six points) and contravening pedestrian crossing regulations (three), then six points would be endorsed. Instead of following this general rule, courts may add the numbers together, making nine points in the example given. However, the court is obliged to give reasons if it adopts this course. The reasons must be announced in open court and be recorded in the court register. Seek advice if necessary: 📖✋

Production of driving licence

When dealing with endorsable offences and following conviction, the court requires production of the offender's licence, if he or she has one. A defendant commits an offence if he or she fails to produce it after the court has required its production. A defence exists if he or she can satisfy the court they have applied for a new licence, but not received it.

Where the court does not receive the driving licence after an order for production, then it is *automatically suspended* from the date the court ordered its production, until it is actually produced. Whilst suspended, the licence is of no effect, and the licence holder, if he drives, will be committing an offence of driving without a licence, on every occasion he or she drives.

'SPECIAL REASONS' FOR NOT ENDORSING

As already indicated, when someone is convicted of an endorsable offence, the court *must* order endorsement and the relevant number of points unless it decides—on the basis of evidence—that there are special reasons for not doing so. The court must state in open court any grounds for finding special reasons, and these must be entered in the court register. A special reason means:

> a mitigating or extenuating circumstance, not amounting to a defence in law, but directly connected with the offence and which the court ought properly to take into account.

Special reasons must relate to the *offence*, as opposed to the *offender*. A special reason within the meaning of the exception is one which relates to the facts of the particular case, i.e. which is special to the facts which constitute the offence. So, e.g. if the offender puts forward the fact that he or she was hitherto of good character and had driven for many years without being convicted of any offence, this would not amount to a special reason in law—since it relates to the offender. The onus is on the offender to establish special reasons and he or she must prove them on a balance of probabilities. Special reasons must be supported by evidence and not mere assertions by the defendant or his or her advocate. If the licence is not endorsed, no points are imposed. Seek advice if necessary: 🕮☝

The court may find that special reasons exist but nevertheless decide not to exercise its discretion in favour of the defendant, having concluded that the special reasons are insufficient to justify this course. Special reasons, when found, are usually unique to the case in question, therefore previous cases/rulings should be used by way of guidance only.

In practice, it is rare for the court to find that special reasons do exist, as a somewhat restrictive interpretation has been adopted by the High Court. Thus, in careless driving cases, it has been held, e.g. that triviality in itself cannot amount to a special reason. The following situations have been accepted by the courts:

- speeding: where the defendant exceeded a motorway speed limit by ten miles an hour, when he was concerned about an elderly passenger who was incontinent and might become ill—he was trying to get to the nearest service area
- using a motor vehicle without third party insurance: a garage proprietor applied for full insurance cover but was issued with a named driver policy without the difference being pointed out to him by the insurance company. In such a situation the defendant must show that in some way he was misled.

In another case, a defendant successfully pleaded special reasons where he executed a U-turn on a motorway across the central reservation. The traffic was blocked on his side of the road. A further example concerned a police officer who successfully pleaded special reasons in an allegation of careless driving when he was responding to an emergency call. Again, it must be emphasised that special reasons can be found but the court still has a discretion to endorse the licence.

Additionally and quite separately to special reasons, under Section 48 Road Traffic Offenders Act 1988 there is a procedure that covers construction and use offences (e.g. defective brakes, tyres, steering) whereby the court cannot endorse if the offender establishes that he or she did not know of and had no reasonable cause to suspect the defect. See *Chapter 6* and seek advice if necessary: 🕮☝

Special reasons and appeals

Where the offender is aggrieved by a decision to order penalty points despite his or her assertion that special reasons exist, there is a right of appeal to the Crown Court or to the High Court on a point of law. The prosecutor also has a right of appeal to the High Court if it is contended that the magistrates' decision on this issue is wrong in law.

Penalty points and fixed penalties

Where an offender has accepted a fixed penalty (below), there is no court hearing. If the offence carries a range of points (such as speeding, i.e. 3-6) the number of points imposed is the lowest in the range.

DVLA PRINTOUTS

After conviction and before sentence for any road traffic offence carrying endorsement, the court should obtain either the defendant's driving licence or a printout of the defendant's driving record. Printouts are necessary in all cases where the defendant's licence cannot be obtained—or one has not been issued. They are obtained from the Driver and Vehicle Licensing Authority (DVLA), Swansea, and contain details of any endorsable offences that an individual has been convicted of and a note of any driving disqualifications. The printout also shows the sentences and court details: see the specimen on page 26.

Some courts operate a 'magnetic tape interchange' whereby they put the information onto a magnetic tape via computer, then post the tape to the DVLA which transcribes it and sends back the relevant printouts.

Many courts are considering the introduction of landline links to further improve services. This means that the period of any adjournment can be kept short. In other instances, it normally takes about three to four weeks to obtain a printout. However, where a defendant appears before the court in custody, then rather than delay sentencing, a designated officer of the court can apply for an expedited printout by telephone. This will be transmitted to the court by facsimile.

FIXED PENALTIES

Special statutory arrangements exist for the endorsement of licences where a fixed penalty is involved. These are discussed in *Chapter 9.*

REVOCATION OF NEW DRIVER'S LICENCE

The Road Traffic (New Drivers) Act 1995 came into effect in 1997. A principle objective of the Act is to reduce the level of accidents and injuries amongst newly qualified drivers. This is achieved by mandatory revocation *by the DVLA* of a driving licence where a new driver accumulates *six or more* penalty points on his or her driving licence within two years beginning with the day on which he or she first passed a test to drive any class of motor vehicle. Points gained as a learner can be added to points in the probationary period therefore two speeding cases, each with less than six points, either side of the test will do. He or she is then only entitled to hold—and drive in accordance with—a provisional licence until they have passed a re-test. Once he has passed such a test, he is eligible for a licence equivalent to the one revoked.

Although the court does not order the revocation, as a matter of good practice the licence holder should be advised by the court that the penalty points imposed will lead to revocation under the Act. Once notified by the court, the DVLA will send a revocation letter to the defendant which will take effect from 5 days after the date of issue.

The 1995 Act is intended to introduce a road safety measure and magistrates should be alert to the fact that some defendants may encourage them to impose a short disqualification to circumvent that legislation. A short disqualification (which will not result in *any* penalty points being endorsed on the licence or notified to the DVLA) may be more attractive to the defendant than a re-test.

It should be noted that revocation under the above provisions does not prevent possible endorsement and/or disqualification if the new driver commits further offences during the period that his or her licence is revoked. This includes, e.g. the possibility of a disqualification under the totting up provisions (see *Chapter 8*), with the six points which resulted in revocation still standing and counting towards the twelve required for that purpose.

NOTIFICATION OF DRIVING DISQUALIFICATION Many courts issue a notice which *inter alia* informs the defendant as follows:

> **YOU HAVE NOW BEEN DISQUALIFIED FROM DRIVING. YOU MAY NOT DRIVE ANY MOTOR VEHICLE ON A ROAD IN GREAT BRITAIN DURING THE PERIOD OF DISQUALIFICATION. THIS OPERATES IMMEDIATELY AND YOU MUST NOT DRIVE ANY MOTOR VEHICLE AWAY FROM THIS COURT. IF YOU DO DRIVE YOU COMMIT AN OFFENCE WHICH IS PUNISHABLE BY IMPRISONMENT AND FURTHER DISQUALIFICATION. IF YOU HAVE NOT ALREADY DONE SO, YOU MUST PRODUCE YOUR DRIVING LICENCE TO THE COURT WITHOUT DELAY.**
>
> **Interim Disqualification (up to 6 months):** This is intended to last until you are sentenced for the offence of which you have been convicted. Your driving licence is suspended until the interim order ceases. If you are then disqualified for the offence, that disqualification will take effect from the date the interim order was made.
>
> **Disqualification for less that 8 weeks** The effect of the disqualification in your case is that your licence is suspended for the period of disqualification. Your driving licence will be retained by the court so that it may be endorsed. It will be returned to you shortly. THE FACT THAT YOU HAVE YOUR LICENCE BACK DOES NOT ENTITLE YOU TO DRIVE DURING THE PERIOD OF DISQUALIFICATION. Once the period of disqualification has finished, your licence will no longer be suspended and you will be entitled to drive.
>
> **Disqualification for 8 weeks or more:** your driving licence will be sent by the Court to the DVLA at Swansea. You must re-apply for your licence, if is not restored to you automatically. The appropriate fee must be sent and you are advised to quote your driving licence number.
>
> **If you are a High Risk Offender** the court must notify the DVLA. You are a High Risk Offender if you have an alcohol level of 87.5 mg in breath, 200 mg in blood or 270 mg in urine. If so, you will be required to satisfy the Medical Advisors at the DVLA that you do not have an alcohol problem. This also applies if you have received two convictions for drink-driving in 10 years, or have a disqualification for refusing to supply a specimen for analysis.
>
> **If you have been disqualified for two years or less** the court has no power to remove your disqualification before its expiry. Disqualifications for longer than two years have their own special rules, but none of them allows the disqualification to be removed in less than two years.
>
> **Disqualification pending passing a driving test**
> The court may have disqualified you from driving until you have passed an appropriate driving test. This applies whether or not you have previously passed a test. The order may take effect immediately or on the expiration of a period of complete disqualification. Where the Order takes effect immediately, you may drive as soon as you obtain a provisional licence but you must, of course, comply with the conditions of a provisional licence. If you are disqualified for a period and also disqualified until you pass a driving test you cannot take out a provisional licence until the period of ordinary disqualification has elapsed. You must obtain a provisional driving licence and comply with the conditions of a provisional licence. If you are in any doubt whatsoever do not drive until you have sought legal advice or contacted the court which made the order.
>
> If your driving licence is delayed you should contact: Customer Services Enquiry, DVLA, Longview Road, Morriston, SWANSEA, SA6 7JL, telephone 01792 772151.
>
> **NB: Once your disqualification has ended you must obtain your driving licence from DVLA before you drive any motor vehicle.**

Adapted extracts from a notice used in Bedfordshire. The notice first recites formal court and personal details, to which the above acts as an explanation.

CHAPTER 8

Disqualification From Driving

There are two kinds of disqualification:

- a *discretionary* power which applies generally in the case of endorsable offences; and
- *an obligatory* (or *mandatory*) power which applies in the case of
  —a minority of specific offences;
  —certain cumulative offending situations; and
  —under the 'totting up' provisions.

These items, their rules, procedures and tightly drawn exceptions are explained in this chapter.

DISCRETIONARY DISQUALIFICATION

The power to disqualify an offender at the court's discretion exists *whenever* an offence is endorsable. This power should only be used in cases involving bad driving or persistent motoring offences or use of vehicles for the purpose of crime. So, in one case, the High Court quashed an order of disqualification for the theft of a range rover where the effect was to hinder the offender from obtaining employment.

A court considering discretionary disqualification should, as a matter of natural justice, warn the parties what is in mind. A discretionary disqualification may not be imposed for the same offence if the offender is also liable to be disqualified under the penalty points provisions (see *'Totting up,'* below), and will not usually arise where the offence attracts *Obligatory Disqualification* (see under next heading).

OBLIGATORY DISQUALIFICATION

Obligatory (or 'mandatory') disqualification arises due to:

- the nature of the offence (i.e. does the statute governing the offence state that disqualification is obligatory); or
- the cumulative effect of earlier disqualifications; or
- most frequently in practice under the totting up provisions.

Offences for which the offender must be disqualified
There are several offences for which an offender *must* be disqualified (usually for a minimum of one year):

- driving/attempting to drive whilst unfit through drink or drugs
- driving/attempting to drive with 'excess alcohol' in the blood or urine
- failing or refusing to provide a specimen for analysis after driving
- dangerous driving
- aggravated vehicle taking.

In all cases, the court *must* order the defendant to be disqualified for 'such period not less than twelve months' as it thinks fit—unless the court for special reasons (i.e. relating to the offence) thinks fit to order the offender to be disqualified for a shorter period, or not to order a disqualification at all.

The principles affecting special reasons have already been set out in relation to endorsement above—including the requirement to state the grounds for finding any such reasons in open court. Special reasons must not be confused with the totting up provisions where mitigating circumstances may apply: see later this chapter.

It must be emphasised that special reasons must be connected with the offence and not the offender. Accordingly, the professional driver who was driving with excess alcohol, albeit only slightly above the legal limit, cannot plead loss of job as a special reason. This is because it relates to him or her, and not to the offence. Hence, the fact that someone will suffer financial hardship, or that his or her family will suffer serious hardship, cannot be a special reason.

Special reasons in drink-driving cases

There is considerable case law concerning special reasons and drink-driving. Several rulings concern offenders who have urged 'emergency' situations, when the general principles are:

- the degree and character of the emergency, and whether it was acute enough to justify taking a car out; and
- the extent to which alternative transport might have been used, as well as other means of dealing with the emergency.

In *Director of Public Prosecutions v. Bristow, The Times,* 28 November 1996, the Divisional Court said that the key question magistrates should ask themselves when assessing whether special reasons exist is:

> What, in a so-called emergency, would a sober, reasonable and responsible friend of the defendant's, present at the time, but himself a non-driver and thus unable to help, have advised in the circumstances—drive, or not to drive? If there was a real possibility he would advise the defendant to drive, the justices could find special reasons.

In one case, it was held that someone who had taken to drinking Listerine mouthwash in quantity could not claim special reasons, even though he did not know that it contained alcohol (26.9 per cent): *Director of Public Prosecutions v. Jowles, The Times,* 13 December 1997.

Sometimes, shortness of the distance driven is urged as a special reason. Here, the general considerations include:

- how far the vehicle was driven
- the manner in which it was driven
- the state of the vehicle
- whether the driver intended to drive any further
- the road and traffic conditions at the time
- whether any possibilities of danger by contact with other road users, including pedestrians, existed
- the reason why the vehicle was driven.

In one case, the defendant—who had been a passenger after the car rolled from the road into a field—drove it from the field to the road and left it there. It was held that special reasons did exist.

It must be emphasised again that where special reasons are established, it does not follow that endorsement or disqualification is automatically avoided. So, where the defendant drives erratically, or the excess of alcohol is substantial, the justices may wish to consider whether the defendant should have appreciated that he or she was not in a condition in which he should have driven.

Laced drinks

'Laced drinks' are sometimes put forward as special reasons for non-disqualification. The defendant has to show that the drinks were, in fact, laced, and that he or she did not know or suspect that this was the case, and that if the drinks had not been laced his or her alcohol level would not have exceeded the prescribed limit. This will normally require medical or scientific evidence. Where the defendant intends to call such evidence in support of special reasons it is desirable that notice is given to the prosecutor in sufficient time before the hearing, to enable him or her to be prepared to deal with the evidence.

In laced drinks cases the defendant will need to establish that:

- the drink was laced, and
- he or she did not know or suspect that fact, and
- had it not been laced, he or she would not have been above the limit.

So, where a defendant honestly thought that he was drinking a soft drink, but it was laced with alcohol, he might be able to succeed with a special reasons application. In general terms, factors for the court to consider would be how he was driving; his ability to drive; what he was drinking and his tolerance for alcohol; should he have realised he was not fit to drive?

Should the court find that special reasons *are* established, and that they are sufficient to avoid the compulsory disqualification, then there is a requirement to state the grounds for finding any such reasons in open court and these must be entered in the court register. Even here, the licence may still be endorsed with penalty points: seek advice 🕮✋

Cumulative effect of earlier disqualifications

A magistrates' court *must* impose a minimum disqualification of two years on an offender on whom more than one disqualification for 56 days or more has been imposed within three years immediately preceding the commission of the offence, if the offence of which he or she has now been convicted involves obligatory disqualification.

This means that an offender who is convicted of any of the offences listed under the heading *Obligatory disqualification* above and who has, within three years immediately preceding the commission of that offence, been subject to more than one disqualification for a period of 56 days or more, must be disqualified for at least two years.

Along similar lines, where an offender is convicted of a drink/driving offence *committed* within ten years of a previous conviction for such an offence, the minimum period of disqualification is not one year but three—unless the court decides, for special reasons, to reduce this obligatory disqualification, or not to impose one at all: see also *Length of totting up disqualification.*

'Totting up'

In the main, the penalty points system is aimed at the offender who persistently commits relatively minor offences, and who ought to be disqualified because of repeated disregard for the law. Where a driver accumulates 12 or more points within a three year span, he or she must generally be disqualified for a minimum period (usually called a 'totting up' or 'penalty points' disqualification). In totting up, the points to be taken into account are:

- those falling to be endorsed for the offence before the court; and
- any that were endorsed on a previous occasion for offences committed within three years of each other, unless already 'wiped clear' by disqualification under the penalty points system (i.e. previous totting up).

When a court disqualifies the offender under the totting up provisions, no penalty points are endorsed for the current offence.

Length of totting up disqualification

The minimum period of a totting up disqualification is:

- *six months* if no previous disqualification falls to be taken into account; or
- *one year* if one previous disqualification falls to be taken into account; and
- *two years* if more than one previous disqualification falls to be taken into account.

A previous disqualification falls to be taken into account if it was imposed within three years of the latest offence which brought the offender's points total to 12. It need not have been for totting up (it could have been for an offence involving obligatory disqualification such as drink driving). However, it must have been for 56 days or more and must not have been imposed for stealing a motor vehicle, taking without consent, or going equipped for theft.

'Mitigating circumstances'

Under the totting up provisions, the offender must be disqualified for one of the minimum statutory periods set out above unless the court is satisfied that there are grounds for mitigating the normal consequences of conviction and sees fit to disqualify for a shorter period, or not to disqualify at all. The question the court should ask itself is: 'Are the mitigating circumstances sufficient to satisfy us in not disqualifying the offender for not less than six months?' The onus of establishing mitigating circumstances is on the offender—on a balance of probabilities. The mitigating circumstances must be much greater to justify the court in not disqualifying at all, rather than reducing the period. No account may be taken of:

- triviality of offence
- hardship, other than 'exceptional hardship'
- circumstances previously taken into account within the three year period.

Mitigating circumstances must not be confused with special reasons (see *Chapter 7*). Mitigating circumstances are far wider in scope—and, in the ordinary way, they will mainly refer to the *offender*. The exceptional hardship put forward will usually relate e.g. to loss of livelihood if disqualification is imposed. It may also relate to loss of employment of other people dependent on the defendant being able to drive; hardship to his or her own employer and hardship to members of his or her own family. If this plea succeeds and the court reduces the minimum period, or decides not to disqualify, then the offender cannot put forward the same ground again until three years have elapsed. Since mitigating circumstances must be announced in open court and are recorded in the court register, courts can make enquiries as to what grounds were found at an earlier hearing. Ultimately, however, it is for the defendant to show that the mitigating circumstances are not the same as were previously taken into account, where that issue arises.

Under the penalty points scheme only one disqualification is imposed irrespective of the number of offences. In the event of an appeal against one or more of the offences, the disqualification will be treated as having been imposed in relation to each endorsable offence. The Crown Court has power to alter sentences imposed by magistrates for several offences, even if the appeal only relates to one of them.

Theft, taking vehicles without consent and similar offences

As already indicated in *Chapter 6*, the general rule is that there can be no discretionary disqualification unless the offence is endorsable. But courts may impose disqualification in respect of offences of:

- stealing a motor vehicle
- taking a motor vehicle without consent; or
- going equipped for the theft of a vehicle

despite the fact that none of these offences are themselves endorsable.

LENGTH OF DISQUALIFICATION

Generally, long disqualifications are considered counter-productive. By way of example, in one case a motorist aged 23 was convicted of aggravated vehicle taking and dangerous driving. His sentence at the Crown Court was 18 months imprisonment concurrent for each offence and he was disqualified from driving for five years. He had driven with excessive speed and dangerously, in busy Greater London streets and caused damage to another motor vehicle. He had no previous convictions or record of bad driving ability. It was held that the disqualification period was too long, and it was reduced to two years. The Court of Appeal indicated that he was of an age where a long period of disqualification from driving might well have a serious effect on his prospects of employment and he might be unduly tempted to flout a disqualification as lengthy as five years.

DISQUALIFICATION UNTIL A TEST PASSED

When a court convicts an offender of any road traffic offence—for which endorsement is obligatory—it can order the defendant to be disqualified until he or she passes a driving test. (Thus the power would not apply to offences coded UT20, UT 30 and UT 40: see *Appendix B*). As long as there is no other disqualification in force, the defendant is entitled to drive a car but must display 'L-plates' and be supervised. If he or she drives without L-plates or supervision, then a charge of driving whilst disqualified can be brought.

The Court of Appeal has repeatedly emphasised that this type of disqualification is not intended as a punishment—but is to protect the public against incompetent drivers or those who fail to use their driving skills properly. Accordingly, the prime reason for considering such an order is the interests of road safety. Orders will generally be in respect of offenders who, through age, infirmity or the circumstances of the offence, display incompetence. Any court disqualifying someone for a long period of time and having misgivings about the offender's ability when the period expires may wish to also consider imposing a disqualification until the offender passes a test.

When the court convicts an offender of dangerous driving, it is not only obliged to disqualify the offender for a minimum of one year—but it must also order disqualification until a test is passed: the 'extended driving test'. This test is longer and more rigorous than the standard 'L-test', and takes place in a variety of road conditions.

When someone is convicted of an offence involving obligatory disqualification, or is liable to totting up, and the court, in its discretion, decides to order disqualification until the offender passes a test, then the test taken by the offender is the extended driving test.

OTHER CONSIDERATIONS

The rule against consecutive disqualifications
Disqualifications cannot be imposed on the same or a subsequent occasion to run consecutively to each other.

Disqualification in absence after notice
An offender cannot be disqualified in his or her absence without first being given the opportunity after conviction of attending an adjourned hearing. As an alternative, the court may issue a warrant for the arrest of the defendant: always seek legal advice: 🕮 ✋

Commencement of disqualification

Disqualification starts from the moment it is imposed (credit being given by the DVLA for any interim disqualification: see under next heading).

Interim disqualification

Where the court has power to impose immediate disqualification after conviction it also has power to impose an interim disqualification if:

- committing the defendant to the Crown Court for sentence
- remitting to another magistrates' court for sentence
- deferring sentence
- adjourning after conviction.

Accordingly, when e.g. a magistrates' court adjourns after conviction for a pre-sentence report (see generally *Chapter 9*), or a DVLA printout (i.e. a computer record of the licence), it may impose an interim disqualification. The DVLA will reduce by the period of the interim disqualification the length of any disqualification imposed by way of sentence at the end of the case. An interim disqualification will automatically last until the case is finalised but, in any event, will not last for more than six months and the court has no power to make a repeat order for the same offence.

REHABILITATION SCHEMES

Where a defendant is convicted of driving or being in charge when under the influence of drink or drugs, or driving or being in charge with excess alcohol in the blood or urine, or failing to provide a specimen, and is disqualified for a period of not less than 12 months, the court has power to *reduce* the period of disqualification by three months, or where it is for a longer period than 12 months by a period of not more than one quarter of its length—provided that the defendant agrees to participate in a rehabilitation course. Such an order can only be made where:

- the court is satisfied that a place on a course is available
- the offender appears to be 17 years of age or older
- the effect of the order is explained to the offender and that he or she is required to pay the fees for the course before it begins, and
- the offender consents to the order being made.

If the offender completes the course successfully and pays the fees involved, a 'certificate of completion' will be forwarded to the court and the reduced disqualification will take effect. Rehabilitation courses are only available in certain areas of the country.

REMOVAL OF DISQUALIFICATION

Anyone who has been disqualified (except e.g. for an interim period or until they have passed a test) can apply to the court for the removal of the disqualification and, if successful, disqualification may be lifted from a date specified in the order. The offender may apply:

- if the disqualification was for less than four years, after two years
- if the disqualification was for less than ten years but not less than four years, when half the period has elapsed
- in other cases, when a period of five years has elapsed.

If the application is refused, the offender must wait at least three months before reapplying. The court should have regard to the character of the offender and his or her conduct subsequent to the offence, the nature of the offence and any other circumstances. The provisions do not differentiate between *discretionary* and *obligatory* disqualification. Many applications concern three year disqualifications for a second drink/driving offence inside ten years. The offender can apply for the return of his or her licence after two years; but case law indicates that magistrates will need a lot of convincing before removing a disqualification which an earlier court was obliged by law to impose.

DISEASE OR PHYSICAL DISABILITY

There is mandatory provision in the Road Traffic Offenders Act 1988 whereby if—in any proceedings for an offence committed in respect of a motor vehicle—it appears to the court that the defendant is suffering from any disability or prospective disability, such as is likely to cause his or her driving to be a source of danger to the public, the court must notify the secretary of state. This may result in the DVLA withdrawing the defendant's driving licence: see *Chapter 9*.

REVOCATION OF NEW DRIVER'S LICENCE

The Road Traffic (New Drivers) Act 1995 came into effect in 1997 and introduced a scheme of mandatory revocation *by the DVLA* of a driving licence where a new driver accumulates *six or more* penalty points on his or her driving licence within two years beginning with the day on which he or she first passed a test to drive any class of motor vehicle: see *Chapter 7*.

THE CRIME (SENTENCES) ACT 1997

A novel power which is extremely wide in its potential application has been introduced on a pilot basis in certain parts of England and Wales in 1998. Section 39(1) of the 1997 Act states that the court may in addition to or instead of dealing with the defendant in any other way, order him to be disqualified, for such period as it thinks fit for holding or obtaining a driving licence. This driving disqualification can be ordered in relation to *any* offence, whether or not connected with driving. The offence need not be an imprisonable one. There is no legal upper limit regarding the period of disqualification.

Courts in the pilot areas will need to consider whether the consequences of the disqualification are commensurate with the seriousness of the offence, e.g. loss of employment and whether the total circumstances would justify this.

DISQUALIFICATION FOR FINE DEFAULT

Another new power introduced by the Crime (Sentences) Act 1997 enables courts in pilot areas to disqualify fine defaulters from driving for up to 12 months (section 40). Defaulters will be able to reduce or totally discharge the period of disqualification by paying some or all of the outstanding monies. In this context fine default include sums owing for costs and compensation.

CHAPTER 9

Sentencing Considerations

Sentencing in road traffic cases is based primarily on the seriousness of the offence (although there may be situations where the protection of the public is the main consideration).[1] Some indications have already been given in earlier chapters of the kind of matters which make a particular offence more serious or less serious: see, e.g. *Chapter 2* in relation to *Dangerous Driving*. The same underlying considerations are likely to affect decisions whether e.g. to disqualify someone from driving where this is discretionary, to disqualify for longer than is mandatory, or what number of penalty points to endorse where an offence attracts a range of points: see, generally, *Chapters 7* and *8*. Influential guidance concerning sentencing is contained in the *Magistrates' Association Sentencing Guidelines*. These include a special section on road traffic offences and this is reproduced in *Appendix A* to this handbook. It is important that the 'Introduction' and 'User Guide' are studied. Not all courts adopt the Association Guidelines, and there are also a number of different ways in which courts take into account the financial circumstances of the offender when imposing a fine: see the examples at the end of this chapter.

DISEASE OR PHYSICAL DISABILITY

Quite apart from sentencing provisions proper, the law seeks to ensure that only fit and competent drivers are allowed on the road. There is a mandatory duty under the Road Traffic Offenders Act 1988 whereby if—in *any* proceedings for an offence committed in respect of a motor vehicle—it appears to the court that the defendant is suffering from any disability or prospective disability, such as is likely to cause his or her driving of a vehicle to be a source of danger to the public, to notify the secretary of state.

---

[1] For a broad overview of the sentencing process—within which the sentencing of road traffic offenders takes place—see *The Sentence of the Court* (Second edition, Waterside Press, 1998). This handbook assumes that a range of considerations as well as the seriousness of the offence come into play according to level of sentence under consideration. See also the comments in this chapter concerning the possibility that the facts of some road traffic offences may bring them within the wide definition of 'violent offence', so that a custodial sentence may be justified in order to protect the public from serious harm from the offender.

There must be sufficient material before the court to support such action, e.g. something said by way of mitigation suggesting that the defendant is suffering from such a disability. But conviction of an offence is not necessary. Accordingly, a court might use this provision where, e.g. a defendant acquitted of careless driving claims that his or her actions were due to a 'dizzy spell', or in respect of someone who is suffering from mental disorder and who is made subject to a hospital order without being convicted. The secretary of state then has various powers including to revoke the licence.

Nature of the requirement

Courts must notify the DVLA if, in any proceedings for an offence, it appears to them that the accused may be suffering from any relevant disability or prospective disability. Generally: 📖 ✋

Relevant disability

A relevant disability is any disability or disease likely to cause the driving of a vehicle by the person concerned to be a source of danger to the public, together with any 'prescribed disability'. Prescribed disabilities include:

- epilepsy
- severe sub-normality
- mental deficiency
- sudden attacks of disabling giddiness or fainting
- inability to pass the eyesight test.

Prospective disability

A 'prospective disability' is one which, because of its intermittent or progressive nature, may become, in the course of time, a relevant disability.

Drink driving

It has been held that a drink problem does not have to be notified to the DVLA, although a high reading (i.e. over 87.5 micrograms in breath), conviction for failing to supply a laboratory specimen, or a second time drink drive offence will result in the offender not receiving his or her licence back at the end of the disqualification period unless the DVLA is satisfied that the individual is medically fit.

Notification to the DVLA

Where a disability exists, the court has no residual discretion whether to notify the DVLA. Once notified of a disability, the DVLA makes its own enquiries and, if satisfied that the defendant is suffering from a

disability may revoke the licence outright or substitute a licence s
to conditions depending on the nature or extent of the disea
disability.

COMPENSATION AND COSTS

There is only a limited power to award compensation where loss or injury arises from a road traffic accident. This power does exist where:

- the damage results from an offence under the Theft Act 1968 such as the unlawful taking of a motor vehicle (i.e. the compensation may relate to the taken vehicle but not damage caused by it); or
- there is injury, loss or damage and:
  —the offender is uninsured in relation to the vehicle; and
  —compensation is not payable under the Motor Insurers Bureau Agreement. This means that, in respect of property damage, the court is restricted to the first £175 of loss not covered by the MIBA (last revised in September 1995). But this may include any reduction in preferential rates, i.e. loss of no claims bonus.

Where a driver is not insured (see *Chapter 4*), financial recompense can become a significant issue. It is important to note the interaction between the MIB and the compensation provisions. If the MIB is liable to meet a claim, then compensation cannot be ordered against an uninsured offender. The MIB will be liable for all injuries with certain limited exceptions (seek advice 🕮 ✋), but as indicated above it is not liable for the first £175 of property damage, nor for any property damage which exceeds £250,000 per accident. It follows, therefore, that in appropriate cases, courts may be asked to make an order for the first £175 of any loss. The MIB can be contacted at 152 Silbury Boulevard, Central Milton Keynes MK9 1NB; telephone 01908 240000.

The compensation provisions

Apart from the special accident arrangements mentioned under the last heading, compensation of up to £5,000 per offence may be ordered to be paid by any person convicted of an offence in addition to any other penalty or order. Such a compensation order can also be a sentence in its own right.

Compensation includes personal injury, loss or damage resulting from an offence for which the offender is convicted or any other offence taken into consideration (TICs). The court in assessing a compensation order must take into account the offender's financial circumstances. Where compensation can be awarded, it must be given priority over a fine. If no order is made in a situation where it could have been, the reason why must be announced by the court.

No application for compensation need be made by the victim/loser and the court may make an order on its own motion. Where an offence is committed under the Theft Act 1968 but the property in question is recovered, any damage which occurred whilst it was out of the owner's possession is treated as resulting from the offence howsoever and by whosoever it was caused.

Compensation orders should only be made in simple and straightforward cases and should enable the offender to complete payment within a reasonable time, normally 12 months. This can be extended where the circumstances justify it.

Civil remedies following an accident

This handbook deals only with the limited powers available to magistrates in *criminal* proceedings. More comprehensive remedies are available in civil proceedings in the county court or High Court where drivers and other people may sue for damages for personal injury or loss resulting from road traffic accidents. The applicant/plaintiff will normally pursue his or her case on the basis of the civil tort of negligence. However, where there has been a conviction in the magistrates' court for dangerous driving or careless driving (*Chapter* 2) this can affect any civil case by assisting a party with what they will need to prove. Evidence of a conviction for careless or dangerous driving is not only admissible in subsequent civil proceedings relating to the same incident, but is *prima facie* evidence of matters decided by the criminal court. The transcript of any evidence given is also admissible.

COSTS

Convicted defendants

Convicted defendants may be ordered to pay so much of the prosecutor's costs as the court considers just and reasonable. The defendant's financial circumstances must be considered and an order should not normally envisage payments over more than a year.

Acquitted or discharged defendants

Magistrates' courts may make orders for costs in favour of acquitted or discharged defendants. Such an order will normally be made unless there are positive reasons for not doing so. These might exist where the defendant's conduct has brought suspicion on himself or herself and has misled the prosecutor into thinking the case was stronger than it is, or where the defendant is acquitted on an unmeritorious technicality.

If a defendant is legally aided a defendant's costs order will only enable him or her to recover those costs not payable under the legal aid order, e.g. travelling expenses. A defendant cannot claim loss of earnings in such circumstances.

Unnecessary or improper acts or omissions ('wasted costs')

Where one party has incurred costs as a result of an unnecessary or improper act, the court may order all or part of the costs to be paid to him or her by the other party. The amount must be specified.

There is also power for wasted costs to be ordered to be borne by a legal or other representative. The court should consider whether there has been an improper, unreasonable or negligent act or omission. It should then consider whether any costs have been incurred as a result thereof, and finally whether the making of an order is an appropriate exercise of its judicial discretion. Advice should be sought: 📖✋

A NOTE ON TICs

The non-statutory practice of defendants asking for outstanding offences—for which they have not been prosecuted—to be taken into consideration (known as TICs) is a means of encouraging offenders to make a clean breast of matters and of disposing of possible further cases easily and quickly. The overall sentence should reflect any TICs and the court should make an appropriate announcement and keep a record of the relevant offences.

Generally speaking, the practice is only appropriate where the court is dealing with more serious, usually either way, offences and it will not be appropriate in the normal course of things to TIC an offence carrying obligatory disqualification or where this would allow the offender to escape the consequences of the penalty points system in due course. If however the principle offence carries disqualification, another offence also involving disqualification might properly be taken into consideration: 📖✋

TOTALITY OF SENTENCE

Courts should consider the overall effect of sentences. It is not uncommon for magistrates to be faced with a long list of traffic offences committed by an individual offender. If, say, a guideline fine were imposed for each an inappropriately high fine would result. It is therefore necessary for the court to review the aggregate sentence in such circumstances. This will usually result in the court restricting its sentence to the most serious offence or offences and imposing 'no separate penalty', nominal fines or absolute discharges in respect of lesser offences. However, the totality principle must not enable an offender to escape the consequences of disqualification.

CUSTODIAL SENTENCES

The general run of traffic offences attract a maximum penalty of a fine. However, a number of the offences described in this handbook are punishable with imprisonment (in addition to those offences dealt with in *Chapter 5, Theft, Taking Without Consent and Like Matters*). Indeed, whether an offence justifies a custodial sentence may be a frequent consideration in relation to more serious varieties of the offences described in *Chapter 3, Offences Involving Drink or Drugs* and dangerous driving (*Chapter 2:* see guidance referred to in that chapter). Offences discussed in this handbook which attract imprisonment include:

- theft of (or damage to) a vehicle
- taking without consent
- aggravated vehicle taking
- dangerous driving
- driving with excess alcohol in the breath, blood or urine (and some associated offences)
- fraudulent use of a VEL (but only in the Crown Court)
- failing to stop/report and accident
- driving whilst disqualified.

The law states that a custodial sentence can only be imposed where:

- the offence (or the offence and one or more offences associated with it) was *so serious* that only such a sentence is justified. Although each case must be judged on its own merits, serious offences, e.g. of dangerous driving and excess alcohol with a high reading are clearly capable of being 'so serious'; or
- where the offence is a violent (or sexual) offence, only such a sentence would be adequate to protect the public from serious harm from the offender. Because of the way in which 'violent offence' is defined, offences such as causing death by dangerous driving, dangerous driving, causing death by careless driving whilst under the influence of drink or drugs, may, on the facts of an individual case, fall into this category: but always It will

not be necessary to rely on this limb of the custody provisions where the offence is, in any event, 'so serious' (above), but in an appropriate case it may justify custody, or a longer custodial sentence than would otherwise be imposed. The provisions in question only apply to custody, not to other forms of sentence.

The need for a pre-sentence report

Before deciding whether the criteria for custody are made out, the court must obtain a pre-sentence report (PSR) unless of the opinion that it is unnecessary to do so. Failure to obtain a report does not invalidate the sentence but any court hearing an appeal must obtain a PSR if the lower court declined to do so (subject to a similar discretion to dispense one).

Legal representation

A custodial sentence cannot be imposed unless the defendant is legally represented or he or she has been offered and has refused or failed to apply for legal aid or has applied for legal aid and this has been refused on the grounds that he or she had adequate means or has been previously sentenced to immediate imprisonment or detention.

Length of a custodial sentence

The length of any custodial sentence should be commensurate with the seriousness of the offence or, as the case may be, the need to protect the public from the offender: 📖✋

Meaning of custody

Offenders aged 21 years and over serve imprisonment. Those under the age of 21 years may be sentenced to detention in a young offender institution. The same provisions with regard to reports and representation apply. However, the minimum sentence for 18 to 21 year olds is 21 days (and, in the youth court, for those aged 15 to 17 years, two months). Detention cannot be suspended: see next heading.

Suspended sentences

Sentences of imprisonment of two years or less may be suspended for one to two years provided that there are *exceptional circumstances* for taking this course. Good character, youth and an early plea of guilty are not exceptional circumstances. Terminal illness and extreme provocation are examples of cases which have been held to be capable of amounting to exceptional circumstances: 📖✋

COMMUNITY SENTENCES

Again, community sentences are unusual in run-of-the-mill road traffic cases either for reasons of legality or practicality. Certain community sentences can only be made where the offence is imprisonable and so can only be used in relation to the offences already listed under the heading *Imprisonment/Custody.*

Where the maximum penalty is a fine, only a probation order is available from the menu of community sentences and in most instances this will not be an appropriate sentence either because the seriousness threshold for a community sentence will not have been reached, or because such a sentence will not be suitable for the offender in all the circumstances. Nonetheless, such a sentence may be appropriate in some situations. The six community sentences are:

- probation
- community service
- combination order
- curfew order (not available in all areas of the country)
- attendance centre (under 21 years only)
- supervision order (under 18 years only).

To justify a community sentence, the offence or the combination of the offence and one or more offences associated with it must be 'serious enough' for this. The restriction on liberty must be commensurate with the seriousness of the offence or offences and the order must be the most suitable for the offender.

There is power to insert into a probation order a requirement to receive treatment for drug or alcohol dependency. It should also be noted that many probation areas now run alcohol education or drink-driving offender schemes, including 'rehabilitation schemes'[2] and that a probation order with appropriate conditions attached to it may be used to good effect in these areas. Seek advice locally: 🕮 ✋

FINES

As can be seen from the earlier chapters of this handbook, many road traffic offences are punishable by reference to maximum fines on one of the five standard fine levels. The standard scale is as follows :

Level	**1**	£200
	2	£500
	3	£1,000
	4	£2,500
	5	£5,000

[2] See, in particular, *Drinking and Driving: A Decade of Development* by Jonathan Black, Waterside Press, 1993.

The amount of the fine should reflect the seriousness of the offence but must also take into account the financial circumstances of the offender. If an offender is facing a number of charges the court should have regard to all the circumstances and apply the totality principle (i.e. fix a maximum ceiling across all the offences: see also the comments under the heading *Totality of Sentence* earlier in this chapter), so that the overall level of fine is not too high. Normally, fines should be payable within a year. The offender can be required to give details of his or her financial circumstances and there are penalties for failure to do so when required or for providing false information. Most courts operate a scheme whereby 'means forms' are issued to defendants at an appropriate point in the proceedings.

ABSOLUTE OR CONDITIONAL DISCHARGE

A discharge is a fairly common disposal in relation to traffic cases. Where the court considers that it is inexpedient to inflict punishment (and a probation order is inappropriate), the offender can be given an absolute discharge or a conditional discharge.

A conditional discharge means that if the offender commits no further offence within the period of discharge (up to three years) he or she will not be punished for the offence. If he or she does commit a further offence, they may be sentenced for the original offence. A conditional discharge cannot be made in the defendant's absence because the order must be explained to the offender.

An absolute discharge marks the conviction but no other consequences follow. This will be appropriate where the offence is of a truly minor nature, purely technical, or when there are several offences and a comparatively trivial one requires a residual sentencing disposal (see also the reference to no separate penalty, which may achieve the same result, under the heading *Totality of Sentence* above).

As with other sentences described in this chapter, an order for compensation or costs may be coupled with an order for conditional or absolute discharge.

FORFEITURE

The power to order forfeiture of property has frequently been used in respect of motor vehicles used for criminal purposes. Before making an order the court must have regard to the value of the property and the likely financial effects upon the defendant of the order.

It was held in one leading case that whilst the use of a car to commit the offence of driving whilst disqualified came within the section, the order should be quashed because insufficient consideration had been given to the defendant's personal circumstances.

Orders of forfeiture should only be made if the property was used for the purpose of committing or facilitating the commission of the offence and only in simple uncomplicated cases. In particular, problems can arise over the ownership of vehicles, which may be on hire purchase, leased or subject to some other third party interest: 📖✋

ENDORSEMENT AND DISQUALIFICATION

These items are dealt with in *Chapters 7* and *8* where the circumstances in which penalty points must be imposed and disqualification must or may be used are explained.

Where disqualification is discretionary, or where there are variable points, the court's decision will be based upon the seriousness of the offence or offences. Good practice indicates that it is wrong to inflate a fine just because the offender is not being disqualified (although experience suggests that this does happen). There may, however, be valid circumstances in which financial penalties should be reduced, i.e. if financial or other hardship (over and above financial or other penalties) will result from an order for disqualification. Where appropriate, the penalty should reflect this. Some form of verification may be needed, e.g. a letter from an employer who is no longer prepared to continue that employment or proof that it will now cost the offender more to continue with some unavoidable commitment.

A NOTE ON FIXED PENALTIES

The time, trouble and expense involved in court proceedings can be avoided for some motoring offences by the police offering the alleged offender a fixed penalty ticket. This offer can be accepted by payment of the fixed sum—when that is the end of the matter. If the matter is not dealt with in this way, then the usual result is a prosecution and court hearing in the normal way.

The system extends to a range of motoring offences, from simple parking to some which carry endorsement such as speeding, pedestrian crossing and construction and use offences involving tyres, steering and brakes. Where there is a range of penalty points and the fixed penalty procedure is used, the lowest number of points in the range is endorsed.

The offer of a fixed penalty is a matter entirely for the police. The procedure depends on whether the offence is endorsable or not.

Offence not endorsable

A police constable (here a traffic warden may perform the duties of a constable) hands a fixed penalty ticket to the driver or, if the driver is absent, attaches it to the vehicle. The defendant has to pay the fixed penalty within 21 days to the relevant justices' clerk (or within such longer period as is allowed by the ticket). The amount of a fixed penalty is such amount as the secretary of state may prescribe. The present levels are:

- £40 for offences involving obligatory endorsement
- £20 for illegal parking (other than in London) and for all other non endorsable offences
- £40 for illegal parking on a Red Route (particularly busy areas in London)
- £30 for illegal parking in London (outside Red Routes).

If payment is made within the time limit, that is the end of the matter. If not—and no court hearing is requested—the police may serve a 'notice to owner' upon the registered keeper of the vehicle. This provides a fresh opportunity for the fixed penalty to be paid. If it is not paid, various things can happen:

- the person served may request a hearing (proceedings then commence in the normal way); or
- the person served may satisfy the police by means of a statutory statement of ownership that he or she was not the owner of the vehicle at the material time. He or she will then escape liability altogether; or
- if not the driver when the offence occurred, he or she can furnish a statement of ownership together with a statutory statement of facts countersigned by the actual driver. This will enable the police to prosecute the identified driver, if they wish to do so.

Driver present—endorsable offence

The officer requires the driver to produce his or her driving licence. If the driver is not liable to a totting up disqualification, the constable can offer the option of a fixed penalty and invite the defendant to surrender the licence. If the driver does not have his or her licence with them at the time, the constable may issue a provisional fixed penalty notice. The driver then has seven days to produce the notice and missing licence at any police station. If he or she does this and it is confirmed that no totting up disqualification is due, the offender will be given a fixed penalty ticket from that police station.

Requesting a hearing
Whenever there is an offer of a fixed penalty, the defendant can, within the stated time limit, ask for a court hearing. Proceedings are then conducted in the normal way. Whether someone had a 'valid reason' for not accepting a fixed penalty may become a sentencing consideration: see the note in *The Magistrate* mentioned at the start of *Appendix A*.

Non-payment of a fixed penalty
If the penalty is unpaid at the end of the period allowed by the ticket, the fixed penalty (£20 non-endorsable offences and £40 endorsable offences) plus 50 per cent of this amount will be registered for enforcement as a fine at the defaulter's home court.

Conditional offer of fixed penalty
A conditional offer scheme is available for all fixed penalty offences (including those which carry endorsement). This allows the police to issue a notice by post to the registered keeper of the vehicle requiring information as to the identity of the driver.

The conditional offer of a fixed penalty is issued to the person identified by the registered keeper as the driver on the occasion when the offence was detected. Should the keeper fail to give information as to the identity of the driver, he or she commits an offence which is itself endorsable. If the driver wishes to take up the offer, he or she will send his or her driving licence and payment to the fixed penalty clerk named in the notice. He or she will accept payment subject to the driver's licence not disclosing that a totting up disqualification is due.

This relatively new procedure is being phased in—initially only in relation to offences detected by automatic devices.

APPEALS

Anybody who has been convicted and sentenced by a magistrates' court can appeal to the Crown Court against the conviction (unless they pleaded guilty), sentence, or both, or to the High Court on a point of law. The prosecutor cannot appeal against an acquittal (other than to the High Court on a point of law or by way of judicial review), or against what he or she believes to be an over-lenient sentence.

Appeal to the Crown Court
This is the normal method. The convicted person must give notice of appeal within 21 days of being sentenced. This can be extended by the

Crown Court (called 'leave to appeal out of time'). The notice of appeal must set out the details of the conviction and sentence and state the grounds of appeal.

Against Conviction

Appeals against conviction are heard by a judge sitting, usually, with two magistrates (technically there can be up to four magistrates). There is no jury. The case is heard afresh. The Crown Court either upholds the conviction or substitutes an acquittal. If it upholds the conviction it will also reconsider sentence.

Against Sentence

This is also heard by a judge and two magistrates. The Crown Court will hear the facts of the case again and in the light of any new information. It is addressed by the appellant (i.e. the person making the appeal) or his or her legal representative. The Crown Court must consider the question of sentence afresh, forming its own view thereon and on the facts as then presented. It can increase or decrease sentence—but is limited to magistrates' maximum powers of punishment.

Appeal against sentence encompasses such matters as disqualification, the endorsement of penalty points, compensation orders and orders for costs. There is power to suspend a driving disqualification pending appeal: see under *Appeals and disqualification*, below.

Appeal to the High Court (the 'Divisional Court')

The High Court has indicated that magistrates who ignore a settled legal point, or who fail to take advice when it is clearly needed, risk being ordered to pay the costs of any appeal personally.

Appeals on points of law go to the Queen's Bench Division (QBD) of the High Court of Justice—where they are heard by a 'Divisional Court' of the QBD. Many of the cases mentioned in earlier chapters of this handbook are rulings of the High Court and the regularity with which such rulings are required serves to emphasise the need for legal/judicial advice in all but the most straightforward cases. There are three methods of appeal to the High Court:

Case stated

Here, the magistrates state a case for the opinion of the High Court. This involves setting down in writing what facts the magistrates found to exist in the case and saying what law or principles they applied to those facts. The Divisional Court either upholds the magistrates' decision or makes some other order, e.g. quashing the conviction; or ordering the magistrates to rehear the case applying the law correctly. There is a timetable for the various stages. The process starts with an application by *either* party (or other person aggrieved by the decision) for the magistrates to state a case for the opinion of the High Court—which must be made within 21 days of the final decision by the magistrates' court. Magistrates can refuse a 'frivolous' application (a technical term), or ask the applicant to identify the point of law involved, e.g. where they are unable to discern a legal issue which actually bore on the decision.

Judicial review

Anyone who is aggrieved by a decision of magistrates (which can extend beyond the parties to other people with a legitimate interest in the outcome of the case—called *locus standi*) may ask the Divisional Court to review the case to see whether, e.g. the court acted judicially, fairly, without bias, observing principles of natural justice, or whether it adopted the correct procedures.

If it did not, the remedy is one or more 'prerogative orders': *certiorari* to quash a decision; *mandamus* to compel the magistrates' court to act (e.g. by hearing the case in a proper manner); and *prohibition* to prevent magistrates acting in error. The would be appellant must normally, within three months, seek the leave of the High Court to make the application for judicial review.

Declarations

More rare, are applications to the Divisional Court by either party for that court to declare what the law is on a particular point, or what it means. The magistrates' court then acts on the advice given.

Appeals and disqualification

Someone who is disqualified from driving by a magistrates' court may appeal against the order (part of the sentence) and the magistrates' court may, if it thinks fit, suspend the order pending the hearing of the appeal. There is no appeal against refusal to suspend a disqualification but, if the magistrates' court refuses to suspend, application may be made to the Crown Court.

A similar power to suspend also exists when the appeal is to the High Court on a point of law.

Effect of suspending disqualification

If disqualification *is* suspended, the period of the suspension does not count towards the disqualification. Thus if a defendant is, say, convicted of driving with excess alcohol in his or her breath, blood or urine and disqualified for 12 months on 1 June 1998 but immediately appeals and the disqualification is suspended, the period of disqualification will run from when the appeal is heard. If the Crown Court dismisses the appeal on the 1 September 1998, the defendant will be disqualified from then until the 1 September 1999.

Days during which a disqualification runs prior to suspension must be subtracted from the period running from the date of the appeal. Thus if a defendant was disqualified on 1 June 1998 for 12 months and appeals to the Crown Court which on 1 July suspend the disqualification pending appeal and on 10 September hears and dismisses the defendant's case, he or she again becomes disqualified on 10 September and remains disqualified until 10 August 1999.

Rectification of mistakes etc.

The magistrates' court has wide power to rectify mistakes and can re-open a case at any time when it appears that it is in the interests of justice to do so. This is particularly useful, for instance if the defendant is convicted in his or her absence of document offences such as no insurance, having no MOT test certificate or no vehicle excise licence and subsequently provides valid documentation. The procedure is quicker and less expensive than that for an appeal: see further in *Chapter 1* under *Re-Opening of Cases.*

Miscellaneous rights of appeal

The Bail Amendment Act 1993 provides the prosecutor with a right of appeal to a Crown Court judge against the grant of bail in certain circumstances by a magistrates' court. Generally, the right only applies where the accused has been granted bail and is charged with any offence punishable by a term of imprisonment of five years or more or an offence under section 12 Theft Act 1968 (taking without consent) or section 12A (aggravated vehicle-taking).

An appeal may only be made if bail was opposed. Oral notice of appeal must be given immediately and written notice must follow within two hours of the conclusion of the hearing. Where notice has been lodged, the accused will remain in custody. The appeal is a re-hearing and must, subject to weekends and Bank Holidays, be heard within 48 hours.

Appendix A

THE MAGISTRATES' ASSOCIATION

SENTENCING GUIDELINES

This edition of the Magistrates' Association Sentencing Guidelines has been produced in consultation with Stipendiary Magistrates and the Justices' Clerks' Society. Grateful thanks go to all those involved in this unique collaboration.

The Sentencing Guidelines are issued with the blessing of the Lord Chancellor and the Lord Chief Justice. The Guidelines are endorsed by the Justices' Clerks' Society.

Mrs A. R. Fuller
Chairman of Council

'I think it most important that, within discretionary limits, magistrates' courts up and down the country should endeavour to approach sentencing with a measure of consistency, and I have no doubt that these guidelines will contribute powerfully to that end.'

The Rt. Hon. The Lord Bingham of Cornhill
Lord Chief Justice of England

Editorial note Reproduced in this *Appendix* are guidelines relating to road traffic offences and other offences described in this handbook. The important 'User Guide' and section on 'Compensation Orders' are reproduced in full, even though of more general application. A note: 'Road Traffic Offences: Penalties' appears at the start of the Road Traffic Guidelines. Some guidelines refer to valid reasons for not paying a fixed penalty (*Chapter 9*). For valuable comment on this aspect see the note by William Miles, Clerk to the Justices at Bracknell, Slough and Windsor which appeared in the March 1998 edition of *The Magistrate*.

Introduction and User Guide

1. Introduction

The Magistrates' Association's *Sentencing Guidelines* cover offences with which magistrates deal regularly and frequently in the **adult criminal courts**. They provide a sentencing structure which sets out how to:

- establish the seriousness of each case
- determine the most appropriate way of dealing with it.

The *Sentencing Guidelines* provide a method for considering individual cases and a guideline from which discussion should properly flow; but they are not a tariff and should never be used as such.

2. Using the sentencing structure

2.1 General principles

Only magistrates decide sentence.

The sentencing structure used was established by the Criminal Justice Act 1991. This re-affirmed the principle of *just deserts* so that any penalty must reflect the seriousness of the offence for which it is imposed and the personal circumstances of the offender. Magistrates must always start the sentencing process by taking full account of all the circumstances of the offence and making a judicial assessment of the seriousness category into which it falls.

In every case, the Criminal Justice Act 1991 requires you to consider:

- is discharge, compensation or a fine appropriate?
- is the offence serious enough for a community penalty?
- is it so serious that only custody is appropriate?

Only when the first assessment of seriousness has been made should offender related mitigation be taken into account. This may not be used to raise the first assessment of seriousness to a higher category; but it may lower it. For example, offender mitigation may bring the seriousness level below the custody threshold into the community sentence range.

2.2 *Establishing the seriousness of the offence*

The guidance for each offence is set for a case of average seriousness and the decision making process involves *establishing the seriousness of the case before the court compared with other offences of the same type*. Users should:

- consider the various seriousness indicators, remembering that some will carry more weight than others.
- make sure that all aggravating and mitigating factors are considered. The lists in the *Guidelines* are neither exhaustive nor a substitute for the personal judgement of magistrates. Factors which do not appear in the *Guidelines* may be important in individual cases.
- always bear in mind that the commission of an offence on bail aggravates its seriousness.
- take care in using previous convictions or any failure to respond to previous sentences in assessing seriousness. We recommend that courts should identify any convictions relevant for this purpose and then consider to what extent they affect the seriousness of the present offence.
- note that when there are several offences before the court, the totality principle requires a court to consider the total sentence in relation to the totality of the offending and in relation to sentence levels for other crimes.

When you have formed an initial assessment of the seriousness of the offence, consider the offender.

2.3 *Using offender mitigation*

The guidelines set out some examples of offender mitigation but there are frequently others to be considered in individual cases. Any offender mitigation which the court accepts must lead to some downward revision of the initial assessment of seriousness, although this revision may sometimes be very minor.

A previous criminal record may reduce offender mitigation.

2.4 *Sentence discount*

The law requires that the court reduces the sentence for a timely guilty plea but this provision should be used with judicial flexibility. A timely guilty plea may attract a sentencing discount of up to one third but the precise amount of discount will depend on the facts of each case and a last minute plea of guilty may attract only a minimal reduction.

Discount may be given in respect of the fine or periods of community service or custody. Periods of mandatory disqualification or mandatory penalty points cannot be reduced for a guilty plea.

2.5 *The available penalties*

2.5.1 *Absolute discharge*

This should be used in the most minor of cases. It acknowledges that an offence has been committed but marks the court's intention to take no further action.

2.5.2 *Conditional discharge*

This is a useful disposal in minor cases where the court needs a sanction which directly discourages further offending.

2.5.3 *Compensation*

Magistrates have the power to award compensation for personal injury, loss or damage up to a total of £5,000 for each offence, including offences taken into consideration; and have a duty always to consider compensation in appropriate cases. When pronouncing sentence you must give an explanation in open court if you decide not to make an award.

Nevertheless, magistrates should not become involved in disputed and complicated cases. Compensation should only be awarded in clear, uncomplicated cases, and the following points need to be borne in mind.

- personal injury need not mean physical injury, eg. an award may be made for terror or distress resulting from an offence.
- compensation may not generally be awarded for injury, loss or damage resulting from a road accident. Consult your clerk for advice in any cases where this point arises.
- where compensation is awarded for damage, the cost of any necessary repairs must be proved to the satisfaction of the court.

In fixing the amount of a compensation order, the defendant's means must be taken into account and the order should normally be payable within twelve months. In exceptional circumstances it may be payable within a period of up to three years; but courts should always consider whether such an extended order is in the interests of the victim.

A table of suggested awards is set out on page viii.

2.5.4 *Fines*

Fines are appropriate for cases which are neither serious enough to attract a community penalty nor so serious that only custody is appropriate. The level of fine for any offence must be commensurate with the seriousness of the offence and must take the offender's means into account

The fine must not exceed the upper limit set by statute for the level of the offence, ie.

For a level 1 offence:	£200
For a level 2 offence:	£500
For a level 3 offence:	£1,000
For a level 4 offence:	£2,500
For a level 5 offence:	£5,000

Before fixing the amount of the fine, the court must enquire into the offender's financial circumstances and we recommend the regular use of means forms.

The Guideline fines in this publication are set at three levels:

Low income	- about £100 net per week from all sources
Average income	- about £250 net per week from all sources
High income	- about £600 net per week from all sources

The fines have not been discounted for a guilty plea.

The principle behind determining the amount of a fine should be that of *equality of hardship rather than equality of monetary penalty*. Punishment does not lie in the amount of a fine but in the degree of hardship and inconvenience caused by the need to pay it. The *just deserts* principle means that each offender should experience the loss of spending power which his or her offending behaviour merits, and levels of fine should always be set with this principle in mind.

Fines are due to be paid at the time they are imposed. Where time to pay is allowed it should not exceed twelve months: in these circumstances best practice should be to order an amount to be paid immediately and then to set a realistic weekly amount, and a date for a court hearing for compliance with the order to be reviewed.

2.5.5 *Community penalties*

Where the offence is *serious enough* a community penalty will be used. They are:

- attendance centre orders (12-36 hours)

- probation orders, with or without special requirements (six months to three years)

- community service orders (40-240 hours unpaid work)

- combination orders (1-3 years probation plus 40-100 hours of community service)

It is good practice always to order a pre-sentence report when a community penalty is under consideration.

The restrictions on liberty imposed by the sentence must be commensurate with the seriousness of the offence and the order must be the one most suitable for the offender. Rehabilitation is a factor to be taken into account in sentencing and a community penalty may be particularly appropriate for this purpose.

2.5.6 Custody

Custody is only appropriate where the offence is so serious that no other form of disposal is justified. It is good practice to order a pre-sentence report before imposing custody.

An offence is so serious that only custody is appropriate when right thinking members of the public, knowing all the facts, would feel that justice had not been done by the passing of any sentence other than a custodial one. R v Cox [1993] 96 Cr. App. R. 452,455.

3. The role of the justices' clerk/court clerk in sentencing

Sentencing is a complex field. Although the decision on sentence rests entirely with the bench, the clerk is under a duty to advise on available sentences and on any case law that may apply to particular types of offence. It is especially important to ask for advice when the bench is considering imposing a custodial sentence.

The clerk's role is described by a Practice Direction issued by the Lord Chief Justice in 1981:

If it appears to him necessary to do so, or he is requested by the justices, the justices' clerk has the responsibility to ... advise the justices generally on the range of penalties which the law allows them to impose and on any guidance relevant to the decisions of the superior courts and other authorities.

Compensation Orders

Priorities
Compensation is an order in its own right, and should be treated as such - particularly where the offender has insufficient means to pay a fine as well.

Damages
Where compensation is to be awarded for damage to, for example, a window, the cost must be proved or agreed.

Payment by instalments
An order for compensation should normally be payable within 12 months, but this can be exceeded up to a three year limit where the circumstances justify it.

Giving reasons
Section 35, Powers of the Criminal Courts Act 1973 states that
'A court shall give reasons on passing sentence if it does not make (a compensation) order in a case where this section empowers it to do so'.

Powers and limitations
Magistrates have power to award compensation for personal injury loss or damage up to a total of £5,000 for each offence. The compensation may relate to offences taken into consideration. There are exceptions including injury, loss or damage due to a road accident unless the damage results from an offence under the Theft Act 1968 or the offender is uninsured and the Motor Insurers Bureau will not cover the loss - if in any doubt, seek advice from the clerk.

An order for compensation should be considered whether or not there is an application by or on behalf of the victim. An award in the magistrates' court will not preclude a civil claim. 'Personal injury' need not be a physical injury. An award can be made, eg. for terror or distress caused by the offence.

Criminal Injuries Compensation Board
The Criminal Injuries Compensation Scheme is intended to compensate victims of violent crime and particularly those who are seriously injured. The minimum award is currently £1,000. Courts are encouraged to order offenders to compensate the victim whether or not the injury comes within the scope of the Criminal Injuries Compensation Scheme, in order to bring home to offenders the personal consequences of their actions. To prevent double compensation for the same injury the Scheme provides for an award to be reduced by the amount of any compensation previously ordered by a criminal court.

Suggested compensation
Damages are assessed under two main headings – **general damages**, which is compensation for the pain and suffering of the injury itself and for any loss of facility; and **special damages**, which is compensation for financial loss sustained as a result of the injury - eg. loss of earnings, dental expenses etc. The suggestions given in the table on the following page are for general damages.

The following guidelines are taken from the Home Office Circular issued in August 1993.

The figures below are only a very general guide and may be increased or decreased according to the medical evidence, the victim's sex, age and any other factors which appear to the court to be relevant in the particular case. If the court does not have enough information to make a decision, then the matter should be adjourned to obtain more facts.

	TYPE OF INJURY	SUGGESTED AWARD
Graze	depending on size	up to £50
Bruise	depending on size	up to £75
Black eye		£100
Cut: no permanent scarring	depending on size and whether stitched	£75-£500
Sprain	depending on loss of mobility	£100-£1,000
Loss of a non-front tooth	depending on cosmetic effect and age of victim	£250-£500
Other minor injury	causing reasonable absence from work (2-3) weeks	£550-£850
Loss of a front tooth		£1,000
Facial scar	however small - resulting in permanent disfigurement	£750+
Jaw	fractured (wired)	£2,750
Nasal	undisplaced fracture of the nasal bone	£750
Nasal	displaced fracture of bone requiring manipulation	£1,000
Nasal	not causing fracture but displaced septum requiring sub-mucous resection	£1,750
Wrist	simple fracture with complete recovery in a few weeks	£1,750-£2,500
Wrist	displaced fracture - limb in plaster for some 6 weeks; full recovery 6-12 months	£2,500+
Finger	fractured little finger; assuming full recovery after a few weeks	£750
Leg or arm	simple fracture of tibia, fibula, ulna or radius with full recovery in three weeks	£2,500
Laparotomy	stomach scar 6-8 inches long (resulting from exploratory operation)	£3,500

Aggravated Vehicle-taking

Theft Act 1968 s. 12A as inserted by Aggravated Vehicle-Taking Act 1992
Triable either way - but in certain cases summarily only - consult clerk.
Penalty: Level 5 and/or 6 months
Must endorse and disqualify at least 12 months:

CONSIDER THE SERIOUSNESS OF THE OFFENCE
(INCLUDING THE IMPACT ON THE VICTIM)

GUIDELINE: ➣

IS COMPENSATION, DISCHARGE OR FINE APPROPRIATE?
IS IT SERIOUS ENOUGH FOR A COMMUNITY PENALTY?
IS IT SO SERIOUS THAT ONLY CUSTODY IS APPROPRIATE?
ARE MAGISTRATES' COURTS' POWERS APPROPRIATE?

⊕ CONSIDER AGGRAVATING AND MITIGATING FACTORS

for example (aggravating)

Avoiding detection or apprehension
Competitive driving: racing, showing off
Disregard of warnings eg from passengers or others in vicinity
Group action
Pre-meditated
Serious injury/damage
Serious risk

Offence committed on bail
Previous convictions and failures to respond to previous sentences, if relevant
This list is not exhaustive

for example (mitigating)

Impulsive
No competitiveness/racing
Passenger only
Single incident of bad driving
Speed not excessive
Very minor injury/damage
This list is not exhaustive

CONSIDER OFFENDER MITIGATION

for example

Age, health (physical or mental)
Co-operation with the police
Voluntary compensation
Remorse

CONSIDER YOUR SENTENCE

Compare it with the suggested guideline level of sentence and reconsider your reasons carefully if you have chosen a sentence at a different level. Consider a discount for a timely guilty plea.

DECIDE YOUR SENTENCE

NB. COMPENSATION - Give reasons if not awarding compensation

Remember: These are GUIDELINES not a tariff

Going Equipped for Theft etc.

Theft Act 1968 s.25
Triable either way - see Mode of Trial Guidelines
Penalty: Level 5 and/or 6 months
May disqualify where committed with reference to the theft or taking of the vehicle

CONSIDER THE SERIOUSNESS OF THE OFFENCE

GUIDELINE: ➢

IS COMPENSATION, DISCHARGE OR FINE APPROPRIATE?
IS IT SERIOUS ENOUGH FOR A COMMUNITY PENALTY?
IS IT SO SERIOUS THAT ONLY CUSTODY IS APPROPRIATE?
ARE MAGISTRATES' COURTS' POWERS APPROPRIATE?

CONSIDER AGGRAVATING AND MITIGATING FACTORS

Aggravating (+)	Mitigating (−)
for example Premeditated Group action Sophisticated Specialised equipment Number of items People put in fear Offence committed on bail Previous convictions and failures to respond to previous sentences, if relevant *This list is not exhaustive*	

CONSIDER OFFENDER MITIGATION

for example

Age, health (physical or mental)
Co-operation with the police
Remorse

CONSIDER YOUR SENTENCE

Compare it with the suggested guideline level of sentence and reconsider your reasons carefully if you have chosen a sentence at a different level. Consider a discount for a timely guilty plea. Consider forfeiture.

DECIDE YOUR SENTENCE

Remember: These are GUIDELINES not a tariff

Theft Act 1968 s.12
Triable only summarily
Penalty: Level 5 and/or 6 months
May disqualify

Taking Vehicle without Conser

CONSIDER THE SERIOUSNESS OF THE OFFENCE

(INCLUDING THE IMPACT ON THE VICTIM)

GUIDELINE: ➢

IS COMPENSATION, DISCHARGE OR FINE APPROPRIATE?

IS IT SERIOUS ENOUGH FOR A COMMUNITY PENALTY?

IS IT SO SERIOUS THAT ONLY CUSTODY IS APPROPRIATE?

CONSIDER AGGRAVATING AND MITIGATING FACTORS

for example

- Group action
- Premeditated
- Related damage
- Professional hallmarks
- Vulnerable victim

- Offence committed on bail
- Previous convictions and failures to respond to previous sentences, if relevant

This list is not exhaustive

for example

- Misunderstanding with owner
- Soon returned
- Vehicle belonged to family or friend

This list is not exhaustive

CONSIDER OFFENDER MITIGATION

for example

- Age, health (physical or mental)
- Co-operation with the police
- Voluntary compensation
- Remorse

CONSIDER YOUR SENTENCE

Compare it with the suggested guideline level of sentence and reconsider your reasons carefully if you have chosen a sentence at a different level. Consider a discount for a timely guilty plea.

DECIDE YOUR SENTENCE

NB. COMPENSATION - Give reasons if not awarding compensation

Remember: These are GUIDELINES not a tariff

Theft

Theft Act 1968 s.1
Triable either way - see Mode of Trial Guidelines
Penalty: Level 5 and/or 6 months

CONSIDER THE SERIOUSNESS OF THE OFFENCE

(INCLUDING THE IMPACT ON THE VICTIM)

GUIDELINE: ➢ ***IS COMPENSATION, DISCHARGE OR FINE APPROPRIATE?***
IS IT SERIOUS ENOUGH FOR A COMMUNITY PENALTY?
IS IT SO SERIOUS THAT ONLY CUSTODY IS APPROPRIATE?
ARE MAGISTRATES' COURTS' POWERS APPROPRIATE?

CONSIDER AGGRAVATING AND MITIGATING FACTORS

for example

High value
Planned
Sophisticated
Adult involving children
Organised team
Related damage
Vulnerable victim

Offence committed on bail
Previous convictions and failures to respond to previous sentences, if relevant
This list is not exhaustive

for example

Impulsive action
Low value
This list is not exhaustive

CONSIDER OFFENDER MITIGATION

for example

Age, health (physical or mental)
Co-operation with the police
Voluntary compensation
Remorse

CONSIDER YOUR SENTENCE

Compare it with the suggested guideline level of sentence and reconsider your reasons carefully if you have chosen a sentence at a different level. Consider a discount for a timely guilty plea.

DECIDE YOUR SENTENCE

GUIDELINE FINES		
LOW INCOME	AVERAGE INCOME	HIGH INCOME
£135	£340	£810

NB. COMPENSATION - Give reasons if not awarding compensation
Remember: These are GUIDELINES not a tariff

Vehicle Interference

Criminal Attempts Act 1981 s.9
Triable only summarily
Penalty: Level 4 and/or 3 months

CONSIDER THE SERIOUSNESS OF THE OFFENCE
(INCLUDING THE IMPACT ON THE VICTIM)

GUIDELINE: ➢
IS COMPENSATION, DISCHARGE OR FINE APPROPRIATE?
IS IT SERIOUS ENOUGH FOR A COMMUNITY PENALTY?
IS IT SO SERIOUS THAT ONLY CUSTODY IS APPROPRIATE?

CONSIDER AGGRAVATING AND MITIGATING FACTORS

+	−
for example Group action Planned Related damage Offence committed on bail Previous convictions and failures to respond to previous sentences, if relevant *This list is not exhaustive*	**for example** Impulsive action *This list is not exhaustive*

CONSIDER OFFENDER MITIGATION

for example
Age, health (physical or mental)
Co-operation with the police
Voluntary compensation
Remorse

CONSIDER YOUR SENTENCE

Compare it with the suggested guideline level of sentence and reconsider your reasons carefully if you have chosen a sentence at a different level. Consider a discount for a timely guilty plea.

DECIDE YOUR SENTENCE

NB. COMPENSATION - Give reasons if not awarding compensation

Remember: These are GUIDELINES not a tariff

ROAD TRAFFIC OFFENCES INDEX

*Full page guidelines identified by **

Road Traffic Offences: Penalties

The general approach is set out in the Introduction and User Guide. However, the following notes will be of assistance when using the guidelines for road traffic offences. Always remember that these are GUIDELINES not a tariff.

Disqualification
A short period of disqualification (up to 56 days) leaves any points already on the offender's licence undisturbed. A longer period of disqualification will wipe the licence clean of penalty points.

Variable penalty points
The points awarded for a variable penalty points offence should correspond with the seriousness of the offence.

Penalty points and disqualification cannot be awarded for the same offence and the number of points or the period of disqualification suggested is targeted strictly at the seriousness of the offence and must not be reduced below the statutory minimum.

Discount for guilty plea
As is set out in the Introduction and User Guide, the precise amount of discount for a timely guilty plea will depend on the facts of each case and may be given in respect of the fine or periods of community penalty or custody.

The multiple offender
When an offender is convicted of several offences committed on one occasion, it is suggested that the court should concentrate on the most serious offence, carrying the greatest number of penalty points or period of disqualification.

The application of the totality principle may then result in less than the total of the suggested amounts of fines for the remaining individual offences.

Totting
Repeat offenders who reach 12 points within a period of three years become liable to a minimum disqualification for six months – but must be given an opportunity to address the court and/or bring evidence to show why such disqualification should not be ordered or should be reduced.

From 1 June 1997 new drivers who tot up six points or more during a two year probationary period from the date of passing the driving test (which may include points for offences committed before the test) will revert to learner status until they pass a repeat test.

Goods Vehicles 3.5 tonnes and over, buses and coaches
Penalties for offences relating to vehicles in the category involving operator licensing are now separated and divided into 3.5 tonnes to 7.5 tonnes, and 7.5 tonnes and over. Owners and drivers of such vehicles will normally be in the average or high income scale and, consequently, no low income figure is given. If, exceptionally, low income is applicable, seek documentary evidence and reduce the fine as appropriate.

It is good practice to consult the clerk, especially when issues are complex.

Road Traffic Act 1988 s.3
Triable only summarily
Penalty: Level 4
Must endorse (3-9 points OR may disqualify)

Careless Driving

CONSIDER THE SERIOUSNESS OF THE OFFENCE
(INCLUDING THE IMPACT ON THE VICTIM)

GUIDELINE: ➢ ***IS DISCHARGE OR FINE APPROPRIATE?***

IS IT SERIOUS ENOUGH FOR A COMMUNITY PENALTY?

(PROBATION IS THE ONLY AVAILABLE COMMUNITY PENALTY FOR THIS OFFENCE)

CONSIDER AGGRAVATING AND MITIGATING FACTORS

for example

Excessive speed
High degree of carelessness
Serious risk

Offence committed on bail
Previous convictions and failures to respond to previous sentences, if relevant
This list is not exhaustive

for example

Sudden change in weather conditions
Minor risk
Momentary lapse
Negligible/parking damage
This list is not exhaustive

Remember, injury or damage cannot be ***equated*** with the degree of carelessness but may ***indicate*** it.

CONSIDER OFFENDER MITIGATION

for example

Co-operation with the police
Voluntary compensation
Remorse

CONSIDER YOUR SENTENCE

Endorse (3-6 points OR period of disqualification)
Consider other measures (including disqualification until test passed if appropriate)
Compare it with the suggested guideline level of sentence and reconsider your reasons carefully if you have chosen a sentence at a different level.
Consider a discount for a timely guilty plea.

DECIDE YOUR SENTENCE

GUIDELINE FINES		
LOW INCOME	**AVERAGE INCOME**	**HIGH INCOME**
£75	**£180**	**£450**

Remember: These are GUIDELINES not a tariff

Dangerous Driving

Road Traffic Act 1988 s.2
Triable either way - see Mode of Trial Guidelines
Penalty: Level 5 and/or 6 months
Must endorse and disqualify at least 12 months
Must endorse (3-11 points) if not disqualified
Must order EXTENDED re-test

CONSIDER THE SERIOUSNESS OF THE OFFENCE

(INCLUDING THE IMPACT ON THE VICTIM)

GUIDELINE: ➢

IS DISCHARGE OR FINE APPROPRIATE?
IS IT SERIOUS ENOUGH FOR A COMMUNITY PENALTY?
IS IT SO SERIOUS THAT ONLY CUSTODY IS APPROPRIATE?
ARE MAGISTRATES' COURTS' POWERS APPROPRIATE?

CONSIDER AGGRAVATING AND MITIGATING FACTORS

for example

Avoiding detection or apprehension
Competitive driving, racing, showing off
Disregard of warnings eg. from passengers or others in vicinity
Evidence of alcohol or drugs
Excessive speed
Prolonged, persistent, deliberate bad driving
Serious risk

Offence committed on bail
Previous convictions and failures to respond to previous sentences, if relevant
This list is not exhaustive

for example

Momentary risk not fully appreciated
No alcohol or drugs involved
Single incident
Speed not excessive
This list is not exhaustive

Remember, injury or damage cannot be ***equated*** with the degree of danger but may ***indicate*** it.

CONSIDER OFFENDER MITIGATION

for example

Co-operation with the police
Voluntary compensation
Remorse

CONSIDER YOUR SENTENCE

Endorse licence and disqualfy at least 12 months unless special reasons apply.
Order EXTENDED re-test.
Compare it with the suggested guideline level of sentence and reconsider your reasons carefully if you have chosen a sentence at a different level.
Consider a discount for a timely guilty plea.

DECIDE YOUR SENTENCE

Remember: These are GUIDELINES not a tariff

Road Traffic Act 1988 s.143
Triable only summarily
Penalty: Level 5
Must endorse (6-8 points OR may disqualify)

Driving – no insurance

CONSIDER THE SERIOUSNESS OF THE OFFENCE

GUIDELINE: ➢ ***IS DISCHARGE OR FINE APPROPRIATE?***

IS IT SERIOUS ENOUGH FOR A COMMUNITY PENALTY?

(PROBATION IS THE ONLY AVAILABLE COMMUNITY PENALTY FOR THIS OFFENCE)

CONSIDER AGGRAVATING AND MITIGATING FACTORS

for example

Deliberate driving without insurance
LGV, HGV, PCV, PSV or minicabs
No reference to insurance ever having been held

Offence committed on bail
Previous convictions and failures to respond to previous sentences, if relevant
This list is not exhaustive

for example

Accidental oversight
Genuine mistake
Insurance held but clearly not covering the driver or use
Recently expired insurance
Misled by another's error
Responsibilty for providing insurance resting with another - the parent/owner/lender/hirer
Smaller vehicle, eg. moped
This list is not exhaustive

CONSIDER OFFENDER MITIGATION

for example

Co-operation with the police
Remorse

CONSIDER YOUR SENTENCE

Endorse licence. The court should have regard to the amount of the insurance premium avoided and the means of the offender and carefully consider the option of disqualification. Compare it with the suggested guideline level of sentence and reconsider your reasons carefully if you have chosen a sentence at a different level. Consider a discount for a timely guilty plea.

DECIDE YOUR SENTENCE

GUIDELINE FINES		
LOW INCOME	AVERAGE INCOME	HIGH INCOME
£215 (£300 LGV/PCV)	£540 (£750 LGV/PCV)	£1,300 (£1,800 LGV/PCV)

Remember: These are GUIDELINES not a tariff

Driving while Disqualified by Court Order

Road Traffic Act 1988 s.103
Triable only summarily
Penalty: Level 5 and/or 6 months
Must endorse: (6 points OR may further disqualify)

CONSIDER THE SERIOUSNESS OF THE OFFENCE

IS DISCHARGE OR FINE APPROPRIATE?

IS IT SERIOUS ENOUGH FOR A COMMUNITY PENALTY?

GUIDELINE: ➢ ***IS IT SO SERIOUS THAT ONLY CUSTODY IS APPROPRIATE?***

CONSIDER AGGRAVATING AND MITIGATING FACTORS

for example

Efforts to avoid detection
Long distance drive
Planned, long term evasion
Recently disqualified

Offence committed on bail
Previous convictions and failures to respond to previous sentences, if relevant
This list is not exhaustive

for example

Emergency established
Short distance driven
Single breach
This list is not exhaustive

CONSIDER OFFENDER MITIGATION

for example

Co-operation with the police
Remorse

CONSIDER YOUR SENTENCE

Endorse (6 points OR period of disqualification)
Compare it with the suggested guideline level of sentence and reconsider your reasons carefully if you have chosen a sentence at a different level.
Consider a discount for a timely guilty plea.

DECIDE YOUR SENTENCE

Remember: These are GUIDELINES not a tariff

Road Traffic Act s.5 (1) (a)
Penalty: Level 5 and/or 6 months: Triable only summarily
Must endorse and disqualify at least 12 months: disqualify at least 36 months for a further offence within 10 years

Excess Alcohol (Drive or attempt to drive)

CONSIDER THE SERIOUSNESS OF THE OFFENCE

The level of seriousness and guideline sentence is related to the breath/blood/urine reading

CONSIDER AGGRAVATING AND MITIGATING FACTORS

for example

- Police chase
- Caused injury/fear/damage
- Type of vehicle, eg. carrying passengers for reward/large goods vehicle
- Evidence of nature of the driving
- High reading (and in combination with above)
- Ability to drive seriously impaired

- Offence committed on bail
- Previous convictions and failures to respond to previous sentences, if relevant

This list is not exhaustive

for example

- Spiked drinks
- Moving a vehicle a very short distance

This list is not exhaustive

BREATH	BLOOD	URINE	DISQUALIFY	GUIDELINE	LOW INCOME	AVERAGE INCOME	HIGH INCOME
36-55	80-125	107-170	12 months	FINE	£180	£450	£1,080
56-70	126-160	171-214	18 months	FINE	£240	£600	£1,440
71-85	161- 195	215-260	24 months	FINE	£300	£750	£1,800
86-100	196-229	261-308	24 months	CONSIDER COMMUNITY PENALTY			
101-115	230-264	309-354	30 months				
116-130	265-300	355-400	30 months	CONSIDER CUSTODY			
131+	301+	401+	36 months				

CONSIDER OFFENDER MITIGATION

for example

- Co-operation with the police

CONSIDER YOUR SENTENCE

Compare it with the suggested guideline level of sentence and reconsider your reasons carefully if you have chosen a sentence at a different level. Consider a discount for a timely guilty plea.

DECIDE YOUR SENTENCE

Remember: These are GUIDELINES not a tariff

Issue April 1997

Refuse evidential specimen (Drive or attempt to drive)

Road Traffic Act 1988 s.7(6)
Penalty:Level 5 and/or 6 months: Triable only summarily
Must endorse and disqualify at least 12 months: disqualify at least 36 months for a further offence within 10 years

CONSIDER THE SERIOUSNESS OF THE OFFENCE

GUIDELINE: ➢ ***IS DISCHARGE OR FINE APPROPRIATE?***

IS IT SERIOUS ENOUGH FOR A COMMUNITY PENALTY?

IS IT SO SERIOUS THAT ONLY CUSTODY IS APPROPRIATE?

CONSIDER AGGRAVATING AND MITIGATING FACTORS

for example

Police chase
Caused injury/fear/damage
Type of vehicle, eg. carrying passengers for reward/large goods vehicle
Evidence of nature of the driving
Ability to drive seriously impaired

Offence committed on bail
Previous convictions and failures to respond to previous sentences, if relevant
This list is not exhaustive

for example

Moving a vehicle a very short distance
This list is not exhaustive

CONSIDER OFFENDER MITIGATION

for example

Voluntary completion of alcohol impaired driver course (if available)
Remorse

CONSIDER YOUR SENTENCE

Endorse licence. DISQUALIFY — a minimum period of 18 months is suggested. Examine carefully aggravating/mitigating factors disclosed - do these justify any variation in period of disqualification suggested? If substantial aggravating factors, consider higher fine/community penalty/custody. Compare it with the suggested guideline level of sentence and reconsider your reasons carefully if you have chosen a sentence at a different level. Consider a discount for a timely guilty plea.

DECIDE YOUR SENTENCE

GUIDELINE FINES		
LOW INCOME	**AVERAGE INCOME**	**HIGH INCOME**
£240	**£600**	**£1,440**

Remember: These are GUIDELINES not a tariff

Road Traffic Act 1988 s. 170 (4)
Triable only summarily
Penalty: Level 5 and/or 6 months
Must endorse: (5-10 points OR disqualify)

Failing to Stop
Failing to Report

CONSIDER THE SERIOUSNESS OF THE OFFENCE
(INCLUDING THE IMPACT ON THE VICTIM)

GUIDELINE: ➢ ***IS COMPENSATION, DISCHARGE OR FINE APPROPRIATE?***

IS IT SERIOUS ENOUGH FOR A COMMUNITY PENALTY?

IS IT SO SERIOUS THAT ONLY CUSTODY IS APPROPRIATE?

CONSIDER AGGRAVATING AND MITIGATING FACTORS

for example

Evidence of drinking
Serious injury and failure to stop or remain at scene
Serious injury and/or serious damage

Offence committed on bail
Previous convictions and failures to respond to previous sentences, if relevant
This list is not exhaustive

for example

Believed identity to be known
Failed to stop but reported
Genuine fear of retribution
Negligible damage
No one at scene but failed to report
Stayed at scene but failed to give/left before giving full particulars
This list is not exhaustive

CONSIDER OFFENDER MITIGATION

for example

Co-operation with the police
Voluntary compensation
Remorse

CONSIDER YOUR SENTENCE

Endorse (5-10 points OR period of disqualification)
Compare it with the suggested guideline level of sentence and reconsider your reasons carefully if you have chosen a sentence at a different level.
Consider a discount for a timely guilty plea.

DECIDE YOUR SENTENCE

GUIDELINE FINES		
LOW INCOME	AVERAGE INCOME	HIGH INCOME
£145	£360	£865

Remember: These are GUIDELINES not a tariff

Fraudulent use etc. Vehicle Excise Licence etc.	Vehicle Excise and Registration Act 1994 s.44 Triable either way - see Mode of Trial Guidelines Penalty: Level 5

CONSIDER THE SERIOUSNESS OF THE OFFENCE

GUIDELINE: ➢ ***IS DISCHARGE OR FINE APPROPRIATE?***

IS IT SERIOUS ENOUGH FOR A COMMUNITY PENALTY?

(PROBATION IS ONLY AVAILABLE COMMUNITY PENALTY FOR THIS OFFENCE)

CONSIDER AGGRAVATING AND MITIGATING FACTORS

for example

- Deliberately planned
- Disc forged or altered
- Long term defrauding
- LGV, HGV, PCV, PSV taxi or private hire vehicle

- Offence committed on bail
- Previous convictions and failures to respond to previous sentences, if relevant

This list is not exhaustive

for example

- Impulsive action

This list is not exhaustive

CONSIDER OFFENDER MITIGATION

for example

- Co-operation with the police/DVLA
- Remorse

CONSIDER YOUR SENTENCE

Compare it with the suggested guideline level of sentence and reconsider your reasons carefully if you have chosen a sentence at a different level. Consider a discount for a timely guilty plea.

DECIDE YOUR SENTENCE

GUIDELINE FINES		
LOW INCOME	AVERAGE INCOME	HIGH INCOME
£100	£240	£575

Remember: These are GUIDELINES not a tariff

Road Traffic Act 1984 s.89(1)
Triable only summarily
Penalty: Level 3 (Level 4 if motorway)
Must endorse (3-6 points OR may disqualify)

Speeding

CONSIDER THE SERIOUSNESS OF THE OFFENCE

GUIDELINE: ➢ ***IS DISCHARGE OR FINE APPROPRIATE?***

CONSIDER AGGRAVATING AND MITIGATING FACTORS

for example

LGV, HGV, PCV, PSV or minicab
Location/time of day/visibility
Serious risk
Towing caravan/trailer

Offence committed on bail
Previous convictions and failures to respond to previous sentences, if relevant
This list is not exhaustive

for example

Emergency established
Limit change (eg. 40 to 30 mph)
This list is not exhaustive

			GUIDELINE FINES		
GUIDELINE PENALTY POINTS	**LEGAL SPEED LIMITS**	**EXCESS SPEED — MPH**	**LOW INCOME**	**AVERAGE INCOME**	**HIGH INCOME**
3	20-30 mph 40-50 mph 60-70 mph	Up to 10 mph Up to 15 mph Up to 20 mph	£60	£150	£360
4 or 5	20-30 mph 40-50 mph 60-70 mph	From 11-20 From 16-25 From 21-30	£90	£225	£540
6 or disqualify (14-56 days)	20-30 mph 40-50 mph 60-70 mph	From 21-30 From 26-35 From 31-40	£135	£335	£810

CONSIDER OFFENDER MITIGATION

for example

Co-operation with the police
Fixed penalty not taken up for valid reason

CONSIDER YOUR SENTENCE

Endorse (3-6 points OR period of disqualification)
Consider other measures (including disqualification until test passed if appropriate)
Compare it with the suggested guideline level of sentence and reconsider your reasons carefully if you have chosen a sentence at a different level.
Consider a discount for a timely guilty plea.

DECIDE YOUR SENTENCE

Remember: These are GUIDELINES not a tariff

Offences considered appropriate for guideline of discharge or fine, other than in exceptional circumstances

	PENALTY POINTS	MAXIMUM PENALTY	LOW INCOME	AVERAGE INCOME	HIGH INCOME
ALCHOHOL/DRUGS					
In charge whilst unfit through drink/drugs or refusing evidential specimen **Consider disqualification if evidence of driving or other aggravating factor*	10*	Level 4 and/or 3 months E	£145	£360	£865
Refusing roadside breath test	4	Level 3 E	£75	£180	£450
DOCUMENTS - Fail to produce	-	Level 3	£25	£60	£145
DRIVER					
Not supplying details **If company- owned,use high income fine when unable to apply endorsement*	3*	Level 3 E	£85	£210	£500*
LICENCE OFFENCES					
† No driving licence, where could be covered	-	Level 3	£15	£30	£75
† Excise Licence not displayed	-	Level 3	£15	£30	£75
LIGHTS - Driving without	-	Level 3	£40	£90	£210
OWNERSHIP - Not notifying DVLA of change, etc.	-	Level 3	£60	£150	£360
PARKING OFFENCES					
† Dangerous Position	3	Level 3 E	£60	£150	£360
† Obstruction	-	Level 3	£25	£60	£145
† Pelican/zebra crossing	3	Level 3 E	£60	£150	£360
† Stopping on clearway	-	Level 3	£40	£90	£210
PROVISIONAL LICENCE OFFENCES					
† Not in accordance with licence	3	Level 3 E	£60	£150	£360
TEST CERTIFICATE - Not held	-	Level 3	£40	£90	£210
TRAFFIC DIRECTION OFFENCES					
† Fail to comply with height restriction	3	Level 3 E	£60	£150	£360
† Fail to comply with red traffic light	3	Level 3 E	£60	£150	£360
† Fail to comply with stop sign/double white lines	3	Level 3 E	£60	£150	£360
† Fail to give precedence - pelican/zebra crossing	3	Level 3 E	£60	£150	£360
TRAFFIC OR POLICE SIGNS (non endorsable)					
† Fail to comply	-	Level 3	£40	£90	£210

† All these items are eligible for fixed penalty offer. If fixed penalty was offered, consider any reasons for not taking up and, if valid, fine amount of appropriate fixed penalty and endorse if required, considering whether costs be waived and allow a maximum of 28 days to pay. Or, if fixed penalty refused or not offered, consider whether known circumstances merit any discount for a guilty plea (but not normally below the fixed penalty amount) or if there are aggravating factors which merit increasing the fine.

In all cases, consider the safety factor, damage to roads, commercial gain and, if driver is not the owner, with whom prime responsibilty should lie.

E: Must ENDORSE (unless special reasons) and may disqualify

Remember: These are GUIDELINES not a tariff

Offences considered appropriate for guideline of discharge or fine, other than in exceptional circumstances

	PENALTY POINTS	MAXIMUM PENALTY	LOW INCOME	AVERAGE INCOME	HIGH INCOME
VEHICLE DEFECTS ETC UP TO 3.5 TONNES GROSS VEHICLE WEIGHT					
Defects					
† Brakes/Steering/Tyres (each)	3	Level 4 E	£60	£150	£360
† Loss of wheel	3	Level 4 E	£120	£300	£720
† Exhaust emission	-	Level 3	£40	£90	£240
† Other offences	-	Level 3	£30	£75	£180
Loads, danger of injury by:					
† Condition of vehicle/accessories/equipment	3	Level 4 E	£75	£180	£450
† Purpose of use/passenger numbers/how carried	3	Level 4 E	£75	£180	£450
† Weight, position or distribution of load	3	Level 4 E	£75	£180	£450
† Insecure load	3	Level 4 E	£75	£180	£450
† Overloading or exceeding maximum axle weight	-	Level 5	£75*	£180*	£450*
** Examine carefully evidence of responsibilty for overload and, if commercial gain relates to owner, consider doubling these figures*			**Plus increase in proportion to percentage of overloading**		

† All these items are eligible for fixed penalty offer. If fixed penalty was offered, consider any reasons for not taking up and, if valid, fine amount of appropriate fixed penalty and endorse if required, considering whether costs be waived and allow a maximum of 28 days to pay. Or, if fixed penalty refused or not offered, consider whether known circumstances merit any discount for a guilty plea (but not normally below the fixed penalty amount) or if there are aggravating factors which merit increasing the fine.

In all cases, consider the safety factor, damage to roads, commercial gain and, if driver is not the owner, with whom prime responsibilty should lie.

E: Must ENDORSE (unless special reasons) and may disqualify

Remember: These are GUIDELINES not a tariff

Offences relating to goods vehicles, buses and coaches from 3.5 tonnes up to 7.5 tonnes gross

	PENALTY POINTS	MAXIMUM PENALTY	OPERATOR	DRIVER	
				AVERAGE INCOME	HIGH INCOME
DEFECTS					
Brakes	3	Level 5 E	£600	£200	£480
Steering	3	Level 5 E	£600	£200	£480
Tyres (each)........................	3	Level 5 E	£600	£200	£480
Loss of wheel	3	Level 5 E	£1,200	£400	£960
Exhaust emission	-	Level 4	£375	£120	£300
Other offences	-	Level 4	£300	£100	£240
LOADS					
Condition of vehicle/ accessories/equipment	3	Level 5 E	£750	£240	£600
Purpose of use/number of passengers/how carried	3	Level 5 E	£750	£240	£600
Weight, position or distribution of load	3	Level 5 E	£750	£240	£600
Insecure load	3	Level 5 E	£750	£240	£600
Overloading or exceeding maximum axle weight	-	Level 5	£750*	£240*	£600*
			*Plus increase in proportion to percentage of overloading		
OPERATORS LICENCE					
Not held	-	Level 4	£600	£200	£480
TACHOGRAPH					
Not fitted	-	Level 5	£600	£200	£480
Not properly used	-	Level 5	£600	£200	£480
Falsification/Fraudulent use	-	Level 5	£900	£300	£720

Drivers of these vehicles will normally be in the average or high income scale and, consequently, no low income figure is given. If, exceptionally, low income is applicable, seek documentary evidence and reduce the fine as appropriate.

E: Must ENDORSE (unless special reasons) and may disqualify

Remember: These are GUIDELINES not a tariff

Offences relating to goods vehicles, buses and coaches 7.5 tonnes gross and over

	PENALTY POINTS	MAXIMUM PENALTY	OPERATOR	DRIVER AVERAGE INCOME	DRIVER HIGH INCOME
DEFECTS					
Brakes	3	Level 5 E	£600	£200	£480
Steering	3	Level 5 E	£600	£200	£480
Tyres (each)........................	3	Level 5 E	£600	£200	£480
Loss of wheel	3	Level 5 E	£1,200	£400	£960
Exhaust emission	-	Level 4	£375	£120	£300
Other offences	-	Level 4	£300	£100	£240
LOADS					
Condition of vehicle/ accessories/equipment	3	Level 5 E	£900	£300	£720
Purpose of use/number of passengers/how carried	3	Level 5 E	£900	£300	£720
Weight, position or distribution of load	3	Level 5 E	£900	£300	£720
Insecure load	3	Level 5 E	£900	£300	£720
Overloading or exceeding maximum axle weight	-	Level 5	£900*	£300*	£720*
			*Plus increase in proportion to percentage of overloading		
OPERATORS LICENCE					
Not held	-	Level 4	£750	£240	£600
SPEED LIMITERS					
Not fitted	-	Level 5	£375	£120	£300
Not properly used or incorrectly calibrated	-	Level 5	£450	£150	£360
TACHOGRAPH					
Not fitted	-	Level 5	£600	£200	£480
Not properly used	-	Level 5	£600	£200	£480
Falsification/Fraudulent use	-	Level 5	£900	£300	£720

Drivers of these vehicles will normally be in the average or high income scale and, consequently, no low income figure is given. If, exceptionally, low income is applicable, seek documentary evidence and reduce the fine as appropriate.

E: Must ENDORSE (unless special reasons) and may disqualify

Remember: These are GUIDELINES not a tariff

Motorway Offences

	PENALTY POINTS	MAXIMUM PENALTY	LOW INCOME	AVERAGE INCOME	HIGH INCOME
DRIVING					
† Driving in reverse on motorway	3	Level 4 E	£145	£360	£865
† Driving in reverse on sliproad	3	Level 4 E	£50	£120	£300
† Driving in wrong direction on motorway * Consider disqualification	3*	Level 4 E	£240	£600	£1,440
† Driving in wrong direction on sliproad	3	Level 4 E	£75	£180	£450
† Driving off carriageway - central reservation	3	Level 4 E	£75	£180	£450
† Driving off carriageway - hard shoulder	3	Level 4 E	£60	£150	£360
† Driving on sliproad against no entry sign	3	Level 4 E	£75	£180	£450
† Making U-Turn * Consider disqualification	3*	Level 4 E	£200	£500	£1,200
LEARNERS					
† Learner driver or excluded vehicle	3	Level 4 E	£75	£180	£450
STOPPING					
† Stopping on hard shoulder of motorway	-	Level 4	£50	£120	£300
† Stopping on hard shoulder of sliproad	-	Level 4	£25	£60	£145
THIRD LANE					
† Vehicle over 7.5 tonnes or drawing trailer in third lane	3	Level 4 E	£120	£300	£720
WALKING					
† Walking on motorway or sliproad	-	Level 4	£40	£90	£210
† Walking on hard shoulder or verge	-	Level 4	£25	£60	£145

† *All these items are eligible for fixed penalty offer. If fixed penalty was offered, consider any reasons for not taking up and, if valid, fine amount of appropriate fixed penalty and endorse if required, considering whether costs be waived and allow a maximum of 28 days to pay. Or, if fixed penalty refused or not offered, consider whether known circumstances merit any discount for a guilty plea (but not normally below the fixed penalty amount) or if there are aggravating factors which merit increasing the fine.*

In all cases, consider the safety factor, damage to roads, commercial gain and, if driver is not the owner, with whom prime responsibilty should lie.

E: Must ENDORSE (unless special reasons) and may disqualify

Remember: These are GUIDELINES not a tariff

Appendix B Offence and Endorsement Codes

Penalty Points and Disqualification

Where a court orders a driving licence to be endorsed and/or an offender to be disqualified the details of the offences are coded. The codes appear on driving licences and DVLA printouts: see, generally, *Chapter 7*. The codes are normally abbreviations of the names of offences, eg SP = speeding, CD = careless driving. The offence codes (May 1998) are as follows:

CODE	OFFENCE	POINTS
Offences in Relation to Accidents		
AC10	Failing to stop after an accident	5-10
AC20	Failing to give particulars or to report an accident within 24 hours	5-10
AC30	Undefined accident offence	4-9
Driving Whilst Disqualified		
BA10	Driving whilst disqualified by order of the court	6
BA20	Driving while disqualified as under age	Replaced by LC20 from 1 July 1992
BA30	Attempting to drive while disqualified by order of court	6
Careless Driving Offences		
CD10	Driving without due care and attention	3-9
CD20	Driving without reasonable consideration for other road users	3-9
CD30	Driving without due care and attention or without reasonable	3-9
	consideration for other road users	3-9
CD40	Causing death by careless driving when unfit through drink	3-11*
CD50	Causing death by careless driving when unfit through drugs	3-11*
CD60	Causing death by careless driving with alcohol level above the limit	3-11*
CD70	Causing death by careless driving then failing to provide specimen for analysis	3-11*

CODE	OFFENCE	POINTS
Construction and Use Offences (Vehicles or Parts)		
CU10	Using a vehicle with defective brakes	3
CU20	Causing or likely to cause danger by reason or use of unsuitable vehicle or using a vehicle with parts or accessories (excluding brakes, steering or tyres) in dangerous conditions	3
CU30	Using a vehicle with defective tyres	3
CU40	Using a vehicle with defective steering	3
CU50	Causing or likely to cause danger by reason of load or passengers	Rescinded 1 July 1992
CU60	Undefined failure to comply with construction and use regulation	Rescinded 1 July 1992
Dangerous (Formerly Reckless) Driving Offences		
DD30	Reckless driving	Replaced by DD 40 from 1 July 1992
DD40	Dangerous driving	3-11*
DD60	Manslaughter or, in Scotland, culpable homicide while driving a motor vehicle	3-11*
DD70	Causing death by reckless driving	Replaced by DD80 from 1 July 1992
DD80	Causing death by dangerous driving	3-11*
Drink or Drugs Offences		
DR10	Driving or attempting to drive with alcohol concentration above limit	3-11*
DR20	Driving or attempting to drive when unfit through drink	3-11*
DR30	Driving or attempting to drive then refusing to provide specimen for analysis	3-11* 3-11*
DR40	In charge of a vehicle with alcohol concentration above limit	10
DR50	In charge of a vehicle when unfit through drink	10
DR60	Failure to provide a specimen for analysis (other than driving or attempting to drive)	10
DR70	Failing to provide specimen for breath test	4
DR80	Driving or attempting to drive when unfit through drugs	3-11*
DR90	In charge of a vehicle when unfit through drugs	10

CODE	OFFENCE	POINTS
Insurance Offences		
IN10	Using vehicle uninsured against third party risks	6-8
Licence Offences		
LC10	Driving without a licence	Replaced by LC20 from 1 July 1992
LC20	Driving otherwise than in accordance with a licence	3-6
LC30	Driving after making a false declaration about fitness when applying for a licence	3-6
LC40	Driving a vehicle having failed to notify a disability	3-6
LC50	Driving after a licence has been revoked or refused on medical grounds	3-6
Miscellaneous Offences		
MS10	Leaving vehicle in dangerous position	3
MS20	Unlawful pillion riding	3
MS30	Play street offence	2
MS40	Driving with uncorrected defective eyesight or refusing to submit to eyesight test	3 (See MS70 and MS80)
MS50	Motor racing on the highway	3-11*
MS60	Offences not covered by other codes as appropriate	
MS70	Driving with uncorrected defective eyesight	3
MS80	Refusing to submit to an eyesight test	3
MS90	Failure to give information as to identity of driver in certain cases	3
Motorway Offences		
MW10	Contravention of special roads regulations (excluding speed limits)	3
Pedestrian Crossing Offences		
PC10	Undefined contravention of pedestrian crossing regulations	3 (mainly Scottish courts)
PC20	Contravention of pedestrian crossing regulations with moving vehicle	3
PC30	Contravention of pedestrian crossing regulations with stationary vehicle	3

CODE	OFFENCE	POINTS
	Provisional Licence Offences	
PL10	Driving without L-plates)	Replaced by LC 20 from 1 July 92
PL20	Not accompanied by a qualified person)	
PL30	Carrying a person not qualified)	
PL40	Drawing an unauthorised trailer)	
PL50	Undefined failure to comply with the conditions of a provisional licence)	
	Speed Limits Offences	
SP10	Exceeding goods vehicle speed limit	3-6
SP20	Exceeding speed limit for type of vehicle (excluding goods/passenger vehicles)	3-6
SP30	Exceeding statutory speed limit on a public road	3-6
SP40	Exceeding passenger vehicle speed limit	3-6
SP50	Exceeding speed limit on a motorway	3-6
SP60	Undefined speed limit offence	3-6
	Traffic Directions and Signs Offences	
TS10	Failing to comply with traffic light signals	3
TS20	Failing to comply with double white lines	3
TS30	Failing to comply with a 'stop' sign	3
TS40	Failing to comply with directions of a constable or traffic warden	3
TS50	Failing to comply with a traffic sign (except stop signs, traffic lights or double white lines)	3
TS60	Failing to comply with school crossing patrol sign	3
TS70	Undefined failure to comply with a traffic direction or sign	3
	Offences of Theft or Unauthorised Taking	
UT10	Taking and driving away a vehicle without consent or an attempt thereat (in England and Wales prior to Theft Act 1968 only). Driving a vehicle knowing it to have been taken without consent; allowing oneself to)	no longer endorsable since 1 July 1992

Code	Offence		Points
	be carried in or on a vehicle knowing it to have been taken without consent. (primarily for use by Scottish courts)	)	As above
UT20	Stealing or attempting to steal a vehicle	)	Non-endorsable
UT30	Going equipped for stealing or taking a motor vehicle	)	
UT40	Taking or attempting to take a vehicle without consent. Driving or attempting to drive a vehicle knowing it to have been taken without consent.) Allowing oneself to be carried in or on a vehicle knowing it to have been taken without consent	)	
UT50	Aggravated taking of a vehicle		3-11*

SPECIAL CODE: TT99
Only used to indicate a disqualification under the totting-up procedures.

SPECIAL CODE NE99
Used where points or disqualification still relevant but endorsement no longer applicable.

AIDING, ABETTING, COUNSELLING, PROCURING
Coded as above but with zero changed to 2 eg UT10 becomes UT12.

CAUSING OR PERMITTING
Coded as above but with zero changed to 4 eg PL10 becomes PL14.

INCITING
Coded as above but with zero changed to 6 eg DD30 becomes DD36.

* These offences involve mandatory disqualification except where special reasons are found by the court. The offences then carry 'notional points'—on a range from 3 to 11—ie which are imposed if special reasons *are* found.

Note that the power to disqualify until a test is passed does not apply to non-endorsable offences: *Chapter 8*

Appendix C Notice of Intended Prosecution

A notice of intended prosecution is needed for the following offences:

- dangerous driving
- causing death by dangerous driving
- careless or inconsiderate driving
- leaving a vehicle in a dangerous position
- dangerous cycling
- careless or inconsiderate cycling
- failing to comply with traffic signs or police signals
- speeding
- aiding or abetting any of the above offences.

Seek legal advice as to whether a particular offence is within the relevant statutory provision, since certain offences may be contrary to more than one such provision, e.g. failure to comply with traffic signs: 🕮✋. The following is an example of the statutory notice:

ROAD TRAFFIC OFFENDERS ACT 1988, SECTION 1 AS AMENDED BY THE ROAD TRAFFIC ACT 1991, SCHEDULE 4
NOTICE OF INTENDED PROSECUTION

Dear

In accordance with the requirements of section 1 of the Road Traffic Offenders Act 1988 I hereby give you notice that consideration is being given to prosecuting you/the driver for committing one or more of the following offences arising out of the use of:

- A mechanically propelled vehicle registered number
  A motor vehicle registered number
  A pedal cycle

- Driving a mechanically propelled vehicle dangerously, contrary to section 2 of the Road Traffic Act 1988 as substituted by section 7 Road Traffic Act 1991

- Driving a mechanically propelled vehicle without due care and attention/without reasonable consideration for other users of the road, contrary to section 3 of the Road Traffic Act 1988 as substituted by section 1 Road Traffic Act 1991

- Riding a pedal cycle without due care and attention/without reasonable consideration for other users of the road, contrary to section 29 of the Road Traffic Act 1988 and amended by the Road Traffic Act 1991, schedule 8.

Time and date of offence:

Where offence committed:

The fact that this notice has been sent to you does not necessarily indicate that you will be prosecuted. To comply with the law such a notice must be sent to you within 14 days of an incident which may lead to a prosecution for the offence(s) named. If it is decided not to institute proceedings you will be informed.

Yours faithfully,

Chief Superintendent

Appendix D Mobile Phones and Road Accidents*

* Reproduced from *Justice of the Peace weekly* journal, 28 June 1997 (161 JPN 619), by kind permission of the proprietors.

Any serious road accident is a matter of concern and particular anxiety has been aroused by a number of fatal road traffic accidents linked with the use of mobile phones. A marketing manager, Peter Mills, was imprisoned for six months by Reading Crown Court on May 23 for causing death by dangerous driving. There was a suggestion that he had used a mobile phone shortly before swerving across the road and colliding with another vehicle, although the Judge made it plain that he was being sentenced for bad driving. The recent inquest on *The Times* correspondent, Kate Alderson, found that she was using a mobile phone to obtain directions when she drove out into the path of another vehicle and was killed. There has been a number of other reports of similar incidents in recent months.

The *Highway Code* (para. 43) specifically advises against the use of hand-held telephone or microphone if it will take the person's mind off the road. Drivers should stop instead, if stopping is permitted. The Code is being revised and amendments are to be made in the light of new evidence on the use of mobile phones.

The Parliamentary Question
On May 19, Lord Campbell of Croy asked the Department for the Environment and Transport Minister, Baroness Hayman, in the House of Lords whether the Government would consider making it an offence to use a telephone while driving a vehicle on a road, whether the telephone is held in the hand or not. Baroness Hayman replied:

> I am urgently considering how best to tackle the hazards posed by driving while using a mobile telephone—whether hand-held or hands-free. Recent court cases do show, however, that the police can and do successfully prosecute the offences of dangerous driving, careless driving or failing to exercise proper control of a vehicle that may arise from the use of a mobile phone while driving.

She later added in a press release:

> I recognise the concerns of many about the use of mobile phones in cars and welcome the action already taken by the mobile phone industry to encourage greater road safety. I believe that further action needs to be taken to increase public awareness of the dangers of using a mobile phone

while driving. Drivers need to be better convinced that driving and mobile phones don't mix.

Offences and penalties

In addition to the offences of causing death by dangerous driving and dangerous driving, mention was made of the offences of careless driving and not having proper control of a vehicle. The Government press release issued on the same day as the reply quoted the maximum penalties for these offences. The maximum for careless driving was correctly given as a maximum fine of £2,500 (Level 4) and discretionary disqualification. The maximum penalty for not having proper control contrary to reg. 104 of the Road Vehicles (Construction and Use) Regulations 1986 was given as £2,500 (Level 4) also but that may be misleading as sch. 2 to the Road Traffic Offenders Act 1988 in referring to s.42 of the Road Traffic Act 1988, makes it clear that this maximum only applies if the offence is committed in respect of a goods vehicle or a vehicle adapted to carry more than eight passengers. Otherwise the maximum penalty is £1,000 (Level 3).

There have been previous discussions on the subject of mobile phones and the matter has been noted in the past in this journal. There is a distinction between a hands-free phone, which may be compared to having a conversation in a car or tuning a radio, and the hand-held variety. The hand-held variety represents a double hazard; not only is one hand occupied which should be available for the steering wheel but the driver's attention is distracted as well. Mobile phones serve a useful purpose particularly for women driving alone and no one has suggested banning them altogether. As Lord Campbell indicated, any offence should be in respect of a moving vehicle.

The problem with the present law is that it is not absolutely illegal to use mobile phones as such, although there is a school of thought that any use of a hand-held phone amounts to a failure to keep proper control. The police have difficulties of proof. If the use of the hand-held variety in a moving vehicle were to be prohibited, everyone would know where they stood. An amendment to this effect to the Construction and Use Regulations would only need secondary legislation, but it may be wiser to make any such new offence plainly endorsable and one carrying discretionary disqualification, and this would require an Act of Parliament. From her Parliamentary reply, the Minister appears at present to favour persuasion, but this may not be sufficient.

Index

📖 **Introduction to the Criminal Justice Process** Bryan Gibson and Paul Cavadino. Rarely, if ever, has this complex process been described with such comprehensiveness and clarity *Justice of the Peace* (First reprint, 1997) ISBN 1 872 870 09 0. £12

The following additional introductory handbooks are scheduled for 1998

📖 **Introduction to Prisons** Nick Flynn *et al* **Foreword: Lord Hurd.** In association with the Prison Reform Trust. ISBN 1 872 870 37 6. £12

📖 **Introduction to Criminology** A Basic Guide Russell Pond A lay person's guide written with people working in the criminal justice arena in mind. The basic ideas of criminology and their sources. ISBN 1 872 870 42 2. £12

A selection of other Waterside Press titles

📖 **Criminal Classes** Offenders at School Angela Devlin
If you are in any doubt about the links between poor education, crime and recidivism, read it: Marcel Berlins *The Guardian.* (First reprint, 1997) ISBN 1 872 870 30. £16

📖 **Children Who Kill** Paul Cavadino (Ed.) With contributions by **Gitta Sereny** and others. From the tragic Mary Bell and Jamie Bulger cases to comparable events world-wide. Highly recommended *The Law.* A rich source of information *BJSW.* (1996) ISBN 1 872 870 29 5. £16

📖 **Tackling the Tag** The Electronic Monitoring of Offenders Dick Whitfield
A comprehensive and balanced guide *Prison Report.* Each court library would benefit from a copy *The Justices' Clerk.* (1997) ISBN 1 872 870 53 8. £16

📖 **Interpreters and the Legal Process** Joan Colin and Ruth Morris Weighty and immensely readable *Law Society Gazette.* An extremely practical guide *The Law.* A scholarly work with everyday practical messages for all professionals *Wig and Gavel.* (1996) ISBN 1 872 870 28 7. £12

📖 **Prisons of Promise** Tessa West **Foreword: Sir David Ramsbotham,** Chief Inspector of Prisons. Extremely well-researched . . . Should be seriously considered by the home secretary *Justice of the Peace.* Deserves to be made available to every magistrate *The Justices' Clerk.* (1997) ISBN 1 872 870 50 3. £16

📖 **I'm Still Standing** Bob Turney The autobiography of a dyslexic ex-prisoner, now a probation officer. A truly remarkable book *Prison Writing.* (1997) ISBN 1 872 870 43 0. £12

📖 **Justice for Victims and Offenders** Martin Wright
An informative addition to the excellent Waterside Press series *Vista.* ISBN 1 872 870 35 X. £16